Reprints of Economic Classics

THE ESSENTIAL PRINCIPLES
OF THE WEALTH OF NATIONS

[JOHN GRAY]

THE ESSENTIAL PRINCIPLES

OF THE

WEALTH OF NATIONS

ILLUSTRATED

IN OPPOSITION TO SOME FALSE NOTIONS

OF

DR. ADAM SMITH AND OTHERS

[1797]

THE ADAM SMITH LIBRARY

REPRINTS OF ECONOMIC CLASSICS

AUGUSTUS M. KELLEY · PUBLISHERS
NEW YORK 1969

First Edition 1797

(London: *Printed for* T. Becket, 1797)

Reprinted 1969 by

AUGUSTUS M. KELLEY · PUBLISHERS

NEW YORK NEW YORK 10010

SBN 678 00504 4

LIBRARY OF CONGRESS CATALOGUE CARD NUMBER

68-55725

PRINTED IN THE UNITED STATES OF AMERICA
by SENTRY PRESS, NEW YORK, N. Y. 10019

THE

ESSENTIAL PRINCIPLES

OF THE

WEALTH OF NATIONS,

ILLUSTRATED,

IN OPPOSITION TO SOME FALSE DOCTRINES

OF

DR. ADAM SMITH, AND OTHERS.

———————— Aratro,
Dignus Honos.   VIRGIL.

To labour diligently, and be content, is a sweet life.
                                                ECCLESIAST.

LONDON:

PRINTED FOR T. BECKET, PALL-MALL.

1797.

THE ESSENTIAL PRINCIPLES

OF THE

WEALTH OF NATIONS,

ILLUSTRATED, &c.

THE caufes of the wealth of nations are various, nay even infinite; for it is out of the power of any man, or of any number of men to enumerate every minute circumftance that may ferve to promote the profperity of a ftate. He that employs his time in collecting linen rags for the ufe of the paper maker, contributes to the wealth of his country. He that in making planks fubftituted the faw for the hatchet, and he that fubftituted carts and waggons for fledges and pack-horfes, were great benefactors to mankind, and in this view were entitled to as much praife and as much recompence as the moft fuccefsful general. In fhort, every perfon in fociety, who prefers honeft induftry to idlenefs, promotes in fome degree the wealth of the nation.

The prudent ftatefman, fenfible that it would be a prefumptuous and vain attempt to trace out the million of fmall caufes that contribute to the wealth of nations, applies his attention chiefly to the principal

cipal and moſt eſſential cauſes, and aſſiduouſly endeavours to render theſe cauſes as efficient as poſſible.

The principal and moſt eſſential cauſe of the proſperity of a ſtate is the ingenuity and labour of its inhabitants exerciſed upon the fertility of its ſoil. All other cauſes of the proſperity of a ſtate, united, are not equivalent to this; and it alone affords that revenue upon which a ſtate is to ſubſiſt and accumulate wealth. This truth, Mr. Locke contented himſelf with ſlightly touching upon; and ſince his time Vanderlint, and ſome other Engliſh political writers, have beſtowed ſome notice upon it. But of late years it has been very ſyſtematically, though not correctly, illuſtrated by many celebrated French writers, who on that account are diſtinguiſhed by the name of Political Economiſts. Dr. Adam Smith in his work, entitled an Enquiry into the Nature and Cauſes of the Wealth of Nations, has in my opinion given, (except in one point) a fair and accurate view of the great outlines of that ſyſtem, according to the French writers, with the purpoſe of objecting to ſome material parts of it. As I mean in my preſent diſcourſe to eſtabliſh that ſyſtem, and to correct the errors of the French Economiſts, and of Dr. Adam Smith, it becomes neceſſary for me to lay before my readers, its leading doctrines according to the French writers, which I ſhall endeavour to do, with as much brevity as is conſiſtent with diſtinctneſs.

According to the French Economiſts, the different orders of people who contribute in any reſpect to-

wards

wards the annual revenue of a country are, firſt, the proprietors of land; ſecondly, the cultivators, whom they honour with the peculiar appellation of the productive claſs; and thirdly, artificers, manufacturers, and merchants, whom they degrade, by the humiliating appellation of the barren or unproductive claſs.

The proprietors contribute to the annual revenue, by what they may occaſionally lay out upon the improvement of the land, by which the cultivators are enabled with the ſame capital to raiſe a greater produce. The cultivators or farmers, who form the ſecond claſs, contribute to the annual produce, firſt by their ſtock, and ſecondly by their annual labour and expenditure; for without ſtock, and without daily labour and expence, the farm would not produce. The farm ought to produce to the farmer a reaſonable profit upon both thoſe capitals, and over and above a ſurplus produce, which goes to the landlord under the name of rent; and on account of both theſe profits, this claſs is diſtinguiſhed by the appellation of the productive claſs. 'Till the landlord receives a reaſonable profit upon the primary expences, and the farmer likewiſe a reaſonable profit upon his ſtock and expence, neither the church nor the king can take any thing without occaſioning a diminution of the produce of ſucceeding years.

The original and the annual expences laid out in cultivating the ſoil, are conſidered as the only productive expences. All other expences are in their eſtimation barren or unproductive; conſequently

quently artificers, manufacturers, and merchants, the third order of men, whose labour only replaces the revenue which they consume, are called barren or unproductive. The expence laid out in employing and maintaining them does no more than continue the existence of its own value, and is therefore unproductive. The wealth of society can never in the smallest degree be augmented by artificers, manufacturers, or merchants, otherwise than by their saving and accumulating part of what is intended for their daily subsistence; consequently it is by privation or parsimony alone, that they can add any thing to the general stock. Cultivators, on the contrary, may live up to the whole of their income, and yet at the same time greatly enrich the state; for their industry affords a surplus produce called rent. Nations therefore that like France and England consist in a great measure of proprietors and cultivators, can be enriched by industry and enjoyment. But nations which, like Holland and Hamburg, are composed chiefly of merchants, manufacturers, and artificers, can grow rich only through parsimony and privation.

The unproductive class however is greatly useful to the classes of proprietors and cultivators, for by means of the industry of that class the latter can purchase manufactures, either foreign or domestic, with a much smaller quantity of their own labour, than if they were to slacken in their attention to cultivation, and to attempt either to manufacture or to import them themselves. The industry of merchants, artificers, and manufacturers, though in its

its own nature altogether unproductive, yet contributes in this manner indirectly to increase the produce of the land. It will always be the interest of the cultivators and proprietors to encourage the industry of the unproductive class, because from that encouragement, competition will arise, and consequently more industry will be procured with less recompence; that is, things will become cheaper. It will likewise always be the interest of the unproductive class to encourage cultivators, because the greater the produce which they draw from the ground, the greater will be the employment of that class. The establishment of perfect justice, of perfect liberty, and of a perfect equilibrium, is the very simple secret, which most effectually secures the highest degree of prosperity to all the three classes.

Should a nation of proprietors and cultivators have in the beginning neither artificers, manufacturers, nor merchants, within its own territory, yet it would be found policy in that nation to admit foreign manufactures free of all duties whatever, because it would thereby purchase them with a less quantity of its own produce, and consequently would have a greater surplus produce, which in progress of time, when its lands were all brought into cultivation, would serve as a capital for the employment of artificers and manufacturers at home. These manufacturers though at first probably unskilful, yet by having it in their power to sell their manufactures cheaper than foreigners could, who brought them from a great distance, would in time be able not only to supply their own nation, without

any

any foreign importation, but to carry their own manufactured goods abroad at a cheaper rate than a mere mercantile nation could afford them. But till its lands be all cultivated, it gains more by employing its capital in the cultivation of its lands, than in promoting manufacturing induſtry; for the former gives a real increaſe, or renewal of revenue, which the laſt does not.

This ſyſtem has truth and nature for its foundation; but the French writers not having gone quite to the foundation, have conſequently not given ſuch an explanation of it as is altogether juſt and accurate. Had the French writers traced the Economical ſyſtem to its foundation, they could not have deemed Receivers of land rents, as mere Receivers of rents, a productive claſs in ſociety. What made them ſtop ſhort in their inveſtigations, I ſhall not pretend to ſay; but they have in ſome degree compenſated for their error by intimating that the Church and King are to be ſerved out of thoſe rents. Dr. Smith, however, not perceiving the error of the French writers; but on the contrary, ſuffering it (ſeemingly as an engraftment from them) to pervade the whole of his own enquiry, directs his refutation to the ſound part of the Economical ſyſtem.

Let us now examine in what manner he combats this ſyſtem. His introductory remark is as follows. ' The capital error of this ſyſtem ſeems to lie in its ' repreſenting the claſs of Artificers, Manufacturers, ' and Merchants, as altogether barren and unpro- ' ductive. The following obſervations may ſerve ' to ſhew the impropriety of this obſervation.'

Now

Now what Dr. Smith apprehends to be the capital error of this syftem, I hope to be able moft fatisfactorily to prove to be no error, but a well-founded truth of great political importance. The Economifts we have feen affirm, that no part of the revenue of fociety arifes from manufactures; and as the difcuffing the validity of Dr. Smith's obfervations affords me an opportunity not only of eftablifhing this truth, but at the fame time of fhewing that the revenue of fociety arifes folely from the induftry of the inhabitants, beftowed upon the fertility of the foil, I fhall therefore proceed to the confideration of the Doctor's obfervations. The firft obfervation is in the following words:—' Firft, this clafs (mean-
' ing the clafs of manufacturers) it is acknowledged
' reproduces, annually, the value of its own annual
' confumption, and continues at leaft the exiftence
' of the ftock or capital which maintains and em-
' ploys it. But upon this account alone the deno-
' mination of barren or unproductive, fhould feem
' to be very improperly applied to it. We fhould
' not call a marriage barren or unproductive, though
' it produced only a fon and a daughter, to replace
' the father and mother, and though it did not in-
' creafe the number of the human fpecies; but
' only continued it as before. Farmers and country
' labourers, indeed, over and above the ftock which
' maintains and employs them, reproduce annually
' a neat produce, a free rent to the landlord. As a
' marriage which affords three children is certainly
' more productive than one which affords only two,
' fo the labour of farmers and country labourers is
' certainly

' certainly more productive than that of merchants,
' artificers, and manufacturers. The superior pro-
' duce of the one class, however, does not render
' the other barren or unproductive.'

The whole of this observation of Dr. Smith is nothing but an evasive quibble about the accurate meaning of the word *barren;* and the comparison he has introduced of a marriage, shews most appositely the fallacy of his conclusion, and establishes the great propriety and justness of the sense given by the Economists to the word barren, that is, *not yielding any increase.* The mother of two children certainly could not be called barren; but a marriage that produced only two children may with the utmost propriety be called barren. If for every child that was born, an adult person died, would a desart country ever become populous? Were this to be the case in Botany Bay, and were no new inhabitants to be imported thither, would New Holland ever become a peopled country? Were I to sow 20 bushels of wheat in a field, and at harvest it should only produce 20 bushels, might it not, with the greatest propriety, be called a barren field? I suspect it would be deemed so by every one, and be deserted accordingly. If this field has produced 20 bushels, some vegetation has appeared in it, *but no increase;* for 20 bushels were thrown into it. Therefore a class of men whose labour (though it produces something) produces no more than what was bestowed, in order to effect that labour, may with the greatest propriety be called an *unproductive class.* It would be wasting my readers time, to bestow more words upon

upon this firſt obſervation. I ſhall proceed to the ſecond.

' Secondly, it ſeems upon this account altogether
' improper to conſider artificers, manufacturers, and
' merchants, in the ſame light as menial ſervants.
' The labour of menial ſervants does not continue
' the exiſtence of the fund which maintains and
' employs them. Their maintenance and employ-
' ment are altogether at the expence of their maſters,
' and the work which they perform is not of a na-
' ture to repay that expence. That work conſiſts
' in ſervices which periſh generally in the very in-
' ſtant of their performance, and does not fix or re-
' alize itſelf in any vendible commodity which can
' replace the value of their wages or maintenance.
' The labour, on the contrary, of artificers, manu-
' facturers, and merchants, naturally does fix and
' realize itſelf in ſome ſuch vendible commodity.
' It is upon this account that, in the chapter in
' which I treat of productive and unproductive la-
' bour, I have claſſed artificers, manufacturers, and
' merchants, among the productive labourers, and
' menial ſervants among the barren or unproductive.'

I muſt begin with remarking, that Dr. Smith, in putting the labour of menial ſervants upon the ſame footing with the labour of artificers and manufacturers, has actually misſtated the doctrine of the Economiſts; and in this point only, as I have before noticed. The Economiſts make a diſtinction between the labour that yields an equivalent for expenditure, and the labour that yields no equivalent. This laſt is the labour of menial ſervants, and
the

the first that of artificers and manufacturers; but still they both are with the greatest propriety termed unproductive; though the one be much more so than the other. I shall explain the difference in a few words. It will be allowed, that a field which returns only the seed sown into it, is a barren field. But some ground, such as the sea beach, may possess no vegetative power at all, and may not even return the seed sown into it, consequently would be much more barren than the other. The labour of menial servants is aptly compared to this very sterile ground. But will the greater sterility of one spot entitle ground to be called productive, that actually returns only the seed, but gives no increase? This difference is only a greater or less degree of a *minus*; but will never give a *plus*. The Economists most readily allow that the labour of artificers and manufacturers fixes itself; which the labour of menial servants does not. But from thence does it follow, with any shadow of logick, that the former yields the smallest increase, and consequently can be called productive. Upon this false induction, however, Dr. Smith says, ' It is upon this account that, ' in the chapter in which I treat of productive and ' unproductive labour, I have classed artificers, ma- ' nufacturers, and merchants, among the produc- ' tive labourers, and menial servants among the ' barren and unproductive.' Has he done so on this account? Then, I say, having no other account, he has actually by these words declared a very large portion of his own treatise fallacious; for the error of deeming that productive which is thus plainly

proved

proved to be unproductive, pervades much more than one chapter of his work.

In his third obfervation Dr. Smith pufhes the point a little further, and attempts to fhew that the labour of artificers and manufacturers does not only give an equivalent for the confumption it occafions, but even yields an increafe. 'Thirdly,' he fays, ' it feems upon every fuppofition improper to fay, ' that the labour of artificers, manufacturers, and ' merchants, does not increafe the real revenue of the ' fociety. Though we fhould fuppofe, for example, ' as it feems to be fuppofed in this fyftem, that the ' value of the daily, monthly, and yearly confump-' tion of this clafs was exactly equal to that of its ' daily, monthly, and yearly production, yet it ' would not from thence follow that its labour added ' nothing to the real revenue, to the real value of ' the annual produce of the land and labour of the ' fociety. An artificer, for example, who in the ' firft fix months after harveft, executes ten pounds ' worth of work, though he fhould, in the fame ' time, confume ten pounds worth of corn and ' other neceffaries, yet really adds the value of ten ' pounds to the annual produce of the land and la-' bour of the fociety. While he has been con-' fuming a half yearly revenue of ten pounds worth ' of corn and other neceffaries, he has produced an ' equal value of work, capable of purchafing either ' to himfelf, or to fome other perfon, an equal half ' yearly revenue. The value therefore of what has ' been confumed and produced, during thefe fix ' months, is equal not to ten, but to twenty pounds.

' It

'It is possible, indeed, that no more than ten
' pounds worth of this value, may ever have existed
' at any one moment of time. But if the ten
' pounds worth of corn and other necessaries, which
' were consumed by the artificer, had been con-
' sumed by a soldier, or by a menial servant, the
' value of that part of the annual produce which
' existed at the end of six months, would have
' been ten pounds less than it actually is, in conse-
' quence of the labour of the artificer. Though
' the value of what the artificer produces therefore,
' should not, at any one moment of time, be sup-
' posed greater than the value he consumes, yet at
' every moment of time the actually existing value
' of goods in the market is, in consequence of what
' he produces, greater than it otherwise would be.'

' When the patrons of this system assert that the
' consumption of artificers, manufacturers, and
' merchants, is equal to the value of what they pro-
' duce, they probably mean no more than that
' their revenue, or the fund destined for their con-
' sumption is equal to it. But if they had ex-
' pressed themselves more accurately, and only as-
' serted that the revenue of this class was equal to
' the value of what they produced, it might readily
' have occurred to the reader, that what would na-
' turally have been saved out of this revenue, must
' necessarily increase more or less the real wealth of
' the society. In order therefore to make out some-
' thing like an argument, it was necessary that they
' should express themselves as they have done; and
' this argument, even supposing things actually
'   were

'were as it seems to presume them to be, turns out to be a very inconclusive one.'

I choose to give Dr. Smith's arguments without any abridgment, though they would lose nothing in being expressed in fewer words. His verboseness and ambiguity clearly shew how a man of ability, when overlooking fundamental principles, may speculate upon the surface of things, without ever getting at the kernel. In this third observation we have what, in mercantile accounts, is called a second entry, that is, the same articles stated twice in the same account, which must necessarily occasion a false aggregate, or false conclusion. 'While an artificer,' he says, 'has been consuming a half yearly revenue of ten pounds worth of corn, and other necessaries, he has produced an equal value of work capable of purchasing either to himself, or to some other person, an equal half yearly revenue. The value therefore of what has been consumed and produced, during these six months, is equal not to ten, but to twenty pounds.' Were this true, artificers and manufacturers would certainly be a productive class. But in stating the case with precision, which the Doctor has not done, it will appear that this hocus pocus manner of turning ten into twenty, is like legerdemain tricks in general, a mere deception. The artificer, he means to say, who produces a piece of manufacture, after half a year's work, may sell it for as much as will maintain him a second half year; consequently, though he has consumed only what fed him six months, he may get, by his manufacture, what will feed him

twelve

twelve months. It has totally efcaped Dr. Smith, that the artificer had no right to fell his manufacture, as it was previoufly mortgaged to pay for his firft fix months provifions; for it cannot be prefumed that his firft fix months provifions were given to him gratis. He that furnifhed thofe provifions to him muft be reimburfed; and how is he to be reimburfed? By the piece of manufacture. Confequently the ten pounds ftill remain ten pounds. I will ftate a cafe analogous, and fimilar to that mentioned by Dr. Smith, which will render his falfe conclufion ftill clearer to my reader. Suppofe a farmer has a defire for a good clock, and meeting with a fkilful clock-maker, juft come out of prifon, without a farthing in his pocket, agrees with him on the following terms, namely, to furnifh him with provifions, materials and tools, till he finifh the clock, and to have the clock in return. Would not the clock-maker be deemed a difhoneft perfon, or a fool, if he attempted to difpofe of the clock to any other perfon but the farmer who furnifhed him with provifions.

It is, I think, unneceffary to enlarge further in the refutation of the third obfervation. I fhall only remark, that the fecond argument, that the artificer by his labour muft create an increafe of value, becaufe the menial fervant does not, is equally inconclufive as the firft, and has already been anfwered.

I proceed to his fourth obfervation, which is in the following words: ' Fourthly, farmers and coun-
' try labourers can no more augment, without parfi-
' mony, the real revenue, the annual produce of the
land

'land and labour of their fociety, than artificers, 'manufacturers, and merchants. The annual pro-
'duce of the land and labour of any fociety can
'be augmented only in two ways; either, firſt, by
'fome improvement in the productive powers of
'the uſeful labour actually maintained within it;
'or, fecondly, by fome increaſe in the quantity of
'that labour.'

'The improvement in the productive powers of
'uſeful labour depends, firſt, upon the improve-
'ment in the ability of the workman; and, fe-
'condly, upon that of the machinery with which
'he works. But the labour of artificers and ma-
'nufacturers, as it is capable of being more fubdi-
'vided, and the labour of each workman reduced
'to a greater fimplicity of operation, than that of
'farmers and country labourers, fo it is likewife
'capable of both thefe forts of improvement in a
'much higher degree. In this refpect, therefore,
'the clafs of cultivators can have no fort of advan-
'tage over that of artificers and manufacturers.'

'The increaſe in the quantity of uſeful labour
'actually employed within any fociety, muſt depend
'altogether upon the increaſe of the capital which
'employs it; and the increaſe of that capital again
'muſt be exactly equal to the amount of the fa-
'vings from the revenue; either of the particular
'perfons who manage and direct the employment of
'that capital, or of fome other perfons who lend it
'to them. If merchants, artificers, and manufac-
'turers are, as this fyſtem feems to fuppofe, natu-
'rally more inclined to parfimony and faving than

'pro-

' proprietors and cultivators, they are so far, more
' likely to augment the quantity of useful labour
' employed within their society, and, consequently,
' to increase its real revenue, the annual produce of
' its land and labour.'

Here we have another misconception of the doctrine of the Economists. The *augmentation* of revenue is not, but indirectly, the object of the Economists, though that would be a consequence of their system. Their object is the *production* and *reproduction* of a revenue, which, they affirm, solely arises from the ingenuity and labour of man exercised upon the fertility of the soil. The people of Great Britain, for example, are such great spenders, that they actually waste and consume to the amount of more than eighty millions sterling annually, and the British farmers are so kind to them as annually to *reproduce* the value of the millions spent. Were the farmers to neglect their annual labour, and no supplies were to come from abroad, there would not be a living soul in Great Britain in fifteen or sixteen months after. A hard frost of three or four weeks continuance, we see, fills the streets of London with the poor gardeners begging for a subsistence, as their revenue is then cut off. From this we may draw a conclusion what would be the national misery on the supposition of a twelvemonths frost. The cattle of the farmers would soon be slaughtered or perish. Every horse would die. The landlords receiving no rents would dismiss all their domestics, who finding none to employ them, must starve or quit the kingdom. The farmers

mers and landlords having no income could not pay taxes; would also cease being customers to the shop-keepers, and could not give employment to carpenters, masons, painters, sculptors, gilders, shoemakers, taylors, &c. all of whom would gradually cease being buyers, and thus the misery would descend from the first ranks to the last, till the means of subsistence ceased to all. The supposition of a twelvemonths frost, I acknowledge, seems rather an improbable supposition. But history gives us what may be reckoned nearly equivalent to it, and records also the consequence, namely, extreme misery. We are told that in Judea no rain fell for above three years, and that the people, in consequence of it, were perishing with famine. Mr. Thunberg, a late Swedish traveller, informs us likewise, that in one of the Cape de Verd Islands, it had not rained for three years, and that it was impossible to describe the misery of the inhabitants. It is not worth while to unravel the inconclusive obscurities of the rest of this observation, which is brought in as subsidiary to the first misconception, as they stand and fall together.

Dr. Smith's fifth and last observation is in the following words: 'Though the revenue of the in-
' habitants of every country was supposed to consist
' altogether, as this system seems to suppose, in
' the quantity of subsistence which their industry
' could procure to them; yet even upon this sup-
' position, the revenue of a trading and manufac-
' turing country must, other things being equal,
' always be much greater than that of one without
                                                                    ' trade

'trade and manufactures. By means of trade and
' manufactures, a greater quantity of subsistence
' can be annually imported into a particular coun-
' try than what its own lands, in the actual state
' of their cultivation, could afford. The inhabi-
' tants of a town, though they frequently possess
' no lands of their own, yet draw to themselves by
' their industry such a quantity of the rude produce
' of the lands of other people, as supplies them not
' only with the materials of their work, but with
' the fund of their subsistence. What a town al-
' ways is with regard to the country and its neigh-
' bourhood, one independent state or country may
' frequently be with regard to other independent
' states or countries. It is thus that Holland draws
' a great part of its subsistence from other countries;
' live cattle from Holstein and Jutland, and corn
' from almost all the different countries of Europe.
' A small quantity of manufactured produce pur-
' chases a great quantity of rude produce. A tra-
' ding and manufacturing country, therefore, natu-
' rally purchases with a small part of its manufactured
' produce a great part of the rude produce of other
' countries; while, on the contrary, a country with-
' out trade and manufactures is generally obliged to
' purchase at the expence of a great part of its
' rude produce, a very small part of the manufac-
' tured produce of other countries. The one ex-
' ports what can subsist and accommodate but a
' very few, and imports the subsistence and accom-
' modation of a great number. The other exports
' the accommodation and subsistence of a great
'number,

'number, and imports that of a very few only.
'The inhabitants of the one muft always enjoy a
'much greater quantity of fubfiftence than what
'their own lands, in the actual ftate of their culti-
'vation, could afford. The inhabitants of the
'other muft always enjoy a much fmaller quantity.'

The fame mifconception and inconclufivenefs run through this obfervation as through the preceding. Were the nature of men the fame as that of foreft horfes, who require neither clothing nor houfes, artificers and manufacturers would have no place among them, and cultivators of the ground would be alone required. But as the nature of man differs from that of foreft horfes, artificers and manufacturers are altogether neceffary to him; and who can doubt but that it is better for any fociety which has brought its lands to a high degree of cultivation, to have thofe artificers and manufacturers refiding within its own territory than without that territory. A nafcent ftate has juft as much need of manufactures as an adult ftate; but while it can with little labour draw a great revenue from its lands, and while foreign commerce exifts among men, it will draw thofe manufactures to itfelf from the diftance of a thoufand miles at a cheaper rate than if they were to be made at home. In an adult ftate lands not yielding fuch a furplus of revenue after the expence of cultivation is deducted, the profit from handicrafts and the allurements of fociety attract in a greater degree the attention of men; and confequently artificers increafe, and villages commence, which by degrees fwell into towns.

A na-

A nation then may be said to become more robust, when it abounds with manufacturers as well as cultivators; for manufacturers are in fact a military corps de reserve, and, if I may be allowed the expression, a granary of soldiers. This enables an adult state to be powerful in defending itself; but a nascent state having no such corps de reserve is feeble in self defence, without foreign aid; but to counterbalance this, it, like man in an infant state, grows faster, is not so quarrelsome, and husbands its strength. While the artificers and manufacturers continue their peaceable employments they are fed by the cultivators, and while they are soldiers they are likewise fed by the cultivators; in the former case they return clothing, and the supply of the other necessary wants of man; and in the latter they return defence; but in either case their labour is only an equivalent for their feeding, and no increase of revenue.

If the produce of their labour is to be exported, and their feeding imported, the former, Dr. Smith alleges, may more than purchase the latter, consequently may yield a revenue. Dr. Smith has here broke bounds, and, contrary to his own plan, has stepped out of the agricultural system into the commercial system. But when the question is about the production of a revenue, it is altogether illogical to substitute for that the transfer of a revenue, which all commercial dealings are merely resolvable into. Whatever be the advantage accruing from exports and imports, that advantage is not an increase of revenue, but a transfer of revenue from

A to B. Should a Jew fell a crown-piece for ten fhillings, or a Queen Anne's farthing for a guinea, he would augment his own income, no doubt, but he would not thereby augment the quantity of the precious metals; and the nature of the traffic would be the fame, whether his virtuofo cuftomer refided in the fame ftreet with himfelf, or in France, or in China. What does the word *commerce* imply, but *commutatio mercium*, an interchange of revenues already created, which moft frequently is for the mutual benefit of both dealers, though fometimes more beneficial to the one than the other; but ftill what the one gains the other lofes, and their traffic really produces no increafe.

But fetting afide the great impropriety of thus changing the ftate of the queftion, the Economift is ready to meet Dr. Smith upon his new ground. If we are to take into confideration the profits from foreign commerce, it will be generally acknowledged, that when any two nations interchange their fuperfluity, or merchandize with each other, that nation which produces its fuperfluity with the leaft expence, will, other things being equal, draw the greateft profit from the fale of that fuperfluity. Now in a nation poffeffing a fertile territory, the production of corn, including in that word the other neceffary articles of fubfiftence, is lefs expenfive than the fabrication of manufactures, confequently the exportation of corn is of all other exportations the moft profitable to fuch a nation.

The comparifon of the profit arifing from cultivation with the profit arifing from fabrication, is of so great importance, and so little attended to by those whose minds are wholly intent upon manufactures and foreign commerce, that it merits a particular illustration.

Suppose a gentleman has four favourite servants, a man and his wife, with their two sons, all capable of labour, and places them in one of his old mansions, with an allowance of ten pounds a year to each for subsistence, 'tis plain they would be an annual charge of 40 pounds to that gentleman. But suppose those same four persons to get possession of 50 acres of good soil, which they wish to cultivate, but having no capital are obliged to borrow every thing. The same friendly gentleman, instead of *giving* them this year 40l. *lends* them 40l. and also *lends* them 90 bushels of seed, a plough, harrows, sickles, &c. and the use of two horses. Of the fifty acres they sow thirty, and being exceedingly industrious, from having the full assurance that all they shall earn will be their own, they in harvest reap 630 bushels, or seven grains for one. Now computing those bushels at 630 crowns, or 157 pounds 10 shillings, and allowing the profits arising from the twenty acres in grass to pay for the implements, and the hire and keep of the horses, they are thus by their crop enabled to acquit all their debts. They reimburse the 40 pounds for their subsistence, and the value of the seed, amounting to 22l. 10s. and allow five per cent interest for the loan, making in all 65l. 12s. which leaves them a reserve, or neat profit of 91l. 18s. In this new situation, therefore, instead of being a charge to the gentleman, they are a charge to nobody, have by their

their own labour subsisted themselves, and realized 91 l. 18 s.

They are now in the second year not under the necessity of borrowing; but have a capital of their own fully sufficient for the same enterprize; therefore supposing the same increase in their arable fields as before, they will in this second year have raised a second income of 157 l. 10 s. to which (as their farm was this year stocked at their own expence) twenty pounds at least must be added for the twenty acres in meadow and pasture, making in all 177 l. 10 s. Deducting from this the expence of the third year's enterprize, or about 62 pounds, and supposing their farm to be as productive, as in the two preceding years, they will at their third harvest have realized a second 177 l. 10 s. to which must be added the reserved capital of their second year, or 112 l. 10 s. making in all 290 pounds.

Should the corn the cultivators have produced each year, which amounted to the marketable value of 157 l. 10 s. be sold abroad, the nation by their industry will be a gainer of 91 l. 18 s. annually. Should it be consumed at home, four persons will have thereby subsisted themselves at nobody's expence, and added to the national capital 91 l. 18 s. annually.

My reader will doubtless have observed, that I have omitted mentioning the payment of any rent for the fifty acres. This is a designed omission, (for in the above stated case no payment of any rent is required) as the fifty acres are supposed to be given by the Supreme Benefactor, who expects no rent
for

for them, but thankfulnefs and obedience to his laws. In fact thefe fifty acres reprefent the feventy-three millions of acres poffeffed by the inhabitants of Great Britain, who pay no rent to any one for the territory they occupy; and my cultivators, if there had not been room for them in Great Britain, might have fat down in Kentucky, where they might have had not fifty acres, but one hundred acres, without paying for them any rent whatever. But of the nature of rent I fhall treat by and by.

Let us now examine the profits accruing to the nation from the exportation of manufactures. It has already been fhewn that no man, as a manufacturer, however he may gain himfelf, adds any thing to the national revenue, if his commodity is fold and confumed at home; for the buyer precifely lofes not only what the manufacturer gains, but the amount of the wages, and of the price of the raw materials befides. There is an interchange between the feller and the buyer, but no increafe. Mr. Edwards, in his judicious and elegant hiftory of the Weft Indies, ftates, that annually 22,000,000 pounds weight of cotton is imported into Great Britain, and manufactured into a value of feven millions and a half fterling, by the full employment of 600,000 people. Suppofe this ftatement accurate, then deduct one million for the prime coft of the cotton, and the labouring manufacturers will be found to earn 10l. 16s. each, which is not the half of a ploughman's earnings. From the ftatiftical account of Scotland, vol. vii. publifhed by the very refpectable Prefident of the Board of Agriculture,

culture, it appears that in 1784 the manufactures of the town of Paisley amounted to the value of 579,185l. and gave employment to 26,484 persons. If from the value of the manufactured commodities, we deduct one-fifth for the price of the raw materials, we shall have the sum of 463,350l. which divided among the above mentioned manufacturers, makes the wages of each amount to 17l. 10s. From Mr. Durnford's History of the Town of Tiverton, in Devonshire, it appears that the total value of the manufactures fabricated there, deducting the price of the raw material, and divided among all the manufacturers, allows to each hardly 10l. a year.

The first reflection that arises from these statements is the smallness of the earnings of the manufacturers, which are not much more than those of a common foot soldier. The second reflection is that there appears to be no surplus; for small as the earnings are, yet the aggregate of them all makes up the full value of the fabrications. To supply the want of a surplus, I shall suppose that the master employer takes a profit of 50 per cent upon what he expends in wages, or sixpence in the shilling on each manufacturer's pay; and allowing the average income of each manufacturer to be 16l. a year, that would make the master's annual gains upon each four manufacturers 32 pounds; and if the manufacture is sold abroad, these 32 pounds would be the national profit from four artificers. Even in this light the exportation of the labour of four cultivators appears to be 38 per cent more profitable to the

the nation than the exportation of the labour of four artificers.

This conclusion however is doing but half justice to the cultivator; for upon a more narrow and accurate inspection it will be found, that the 32 pounds which the master employer is enabled to draw from abroad by the sale of his manufacture, is not owing solely to the four manufacturers, but in part to the cultivators, who fed those manufacturers. Had there been no subsistence provided, there would have been no work done; and the value of the work done, we have seen above, does no more than compensate for the value of the subsistence. Therefore to send abroad such a value in manufactures as should yield a profit of 32 pounds to the exporter, requires not the labour of four men only, but of six men, allowing the surplus produce of two cultivators sufficient to feed four manufacturers. Now if six men are necessary to the procuring a profit of 32 pounds by the exportation of manufactures, and four men can procure a profit of 51 pounds by the exportation of corn, the national profit from the exportation of the latter exceeds that from the exportation of the former nearly in the proportion of $2\frac{1}{2}$ to 1. Mr. Jefferson of Virginia therefore speaks the language of an enlightened politician when he says, ' 'Tis for the interest of the American States, that for a long time to come their manufacturers should reside in Europe.'

The preceding reflections, I think, suffice to shew the falseness of Dr. Smith's position, that the exportation of manufactures may create a revenue

to

to a ſtate in preference to the exportation of rude produce. His reaſoning in the reſt of this obſervation, if obſcure ſophiſtry deſerves the name of reaſoning, is equally incluſive with what has been refuted. What has *great quantity* and *ſmall quantity* to do in the compariſon of one value with another value. A ſmall bundle of lace will purchaſe many ſackfuls of corn; but the queſtion is, if food be wanted, or even if gold be wanted, whether the manufacturers of that lace would not have drawn more profit to themſelves and to their country, if they had employed themſelves as cultivators, than as manufacturers; and that queſtion having already been reſolved, ſhews the *nomeaning* of the words great quantity and ſmall quantity.

Dr. Smith further ſays, ' The inhabitants of a
' town, though they frequently poſſeſs no lands of
' their own, yet draw to themſelves by their induſ-
' try ſuch a quantity of the rude produce of the
' lands of other people as ſupplies them not only
' with the materials of their work, but with the
' fund of their ſubſiſtence.' The very terms of this ſentence diſprove what Dr. Smith wiſhes to prove by it. The inhabitants of a town, he ſays, *draw* to themſelves the *rude produce* of other people. By thus drawing it is evident they do not *create* a revenue, but *transfer* the revenue created by others. Who ever doubted that in traffic one may gain and another may loſe? But where the inquiry is not concerning the ſource of the wealth of individuals, but of the Wealth of Nations, it is rather illogical to ſubſtitute the one for the other. Dr. Smith

Smith not adverting to this paralogifm goes on. 'It is thus,' he fays, 'that Holland draws a great part of its fubfiftence from other countries; live cattle from Holftein and Jutland, and corn from almoft all the different ftates of Europe.' Now before any thing can be inferred from this, in favour of his fuppofition, Dr. Smith ought to have proved, that Denmark and Poland are lofers in fupplying Holland with beef and corn in return for manufactures. But from what is above written the prefumption is, that the gain is on the fide of Denmark and Poland, and that thefe kingdoms, while any lands remain in them uncultivated, may adopt the language of Mr. Jefferfon, and fay, 'It is for the intereft of Denmark and Poland, that for a long time to come their manufacturers fhould refide in Holland.'

That the pecuniary wealth of Holland exceeds that of any other European nation has been noticed by many writers; but he muft not have perufed hiftory with much attention who attributes that wealth to the manufactures carried on by the Hollanders. The enquiring Economift will find three much more copious fources of that wealth than manufactures; and two of them that are actually fources of the natural and real revenue, to which wife nations will ever give the preference, namely, territorial improvement and fifhing. When the Economift fays that the chief fource of the wealth of nations confifts in the labour of man exercifed upon the fertility of the foil, he by no means excludes the fertility of the feas, as the ocean, when

ploughed

ploughed by fishermen, yields an increase frequently as abundant as the land when ploughed by husbandmen. By this natural source of wealth the Dutch were formerly, and still are great gainers. The famous De Witt reckoned that one-fourth of his countrymen were maintained by fishing; and the distinguished engineer, Thomas Digges, in Queen Elizabeth's reign, who spent a considerable time in Holland, says, 'Fishinge onlye being none of the leaste 'foundations of all their proude townes, built in our 'age.' (See his plan for improving Dover Haven, written about the year 1582, and printed in the Archæologia, vol. II.) Now if the Dutch territory hardly suffices to maintain one-half of its inhabitants, and one-fourth of them draw their subsistence from fishing, this is nearly the same thing as if their land territory were enlarged one-half, and to be productive of a revenue.

Another source of Dutch revenue is likewise equivalent to an enlargement of land territory; I mean the monopoly of the spices of the East. Were Great Britain to possess a monopoly of the growth of potatoes, and finding a great demand for them in other countries, should sell them at five shillings a pound, instead of a penny a pound, 'tis plain that one acre of potatoes in that case would, in point of mercantile profit, be equal to 60 acres. But such for these two hundred years past has nearly been the case in respect to Dutch traffic in nutmegs, cloves, mace, cinnamon, which are at the tables of the luxurious, what gin is at the meals of the indigent. Were the expence of the production or purchase of those spices in the East, and the

European

European market prices of them to be compared together, they would be found to differ as widely as the pound of potatoes produced at the expence of one penny, and sold for five shillings, differ from each other; and all that difference is so much gain to the monopolizing Dutch, and renders every acre of nutmegs nearly equivalent to 60 acres of corn. Were this monopoly to be permanent, it would be a permanent advantage to the Dutch, an advantage which my readers will perceive is in respect to production a natural revenue, but in respect to mercantile value, only a revenue transferred, distinct however from that arising from manufactures.

The third great source of the opulence of the Dutch, of which likewise they long possessed a kind of monopoly, and which in its nature is distinct from manufactures, is the carrying trade. Their ships were so many floating warehouses and retail shops, appearing in every quarter of the globe, buying cheap in one nation, and selling dear in another, and carrying the wealth thus acquired by transfers of revenue home to their narrow hive at the mouths of the Rhine. Of these three sources of Dutch income; the first, namely, the fishing, is a real new production; the second, arising from the sale of spices, is in part a new production, and in part only a transfer of revenue; and the third is wholly a transfer of a revenue already created, but no new production. Out of these three revenues the parsimony of the Dutch has formed a fourth revenue, which however is no new production, but a revenue drawn to themselves from the revenue of

their

their lefs thrifty neighbours. Thus the whole of the prefent land-tax of Kent and Suffex, and perhaps of Effex, belongs to the Dutch, and goes to maintain Dutchmen in Holland, in confequence of fums lent by them to the Government of Great Britain. The Dutch having long perfevered in this money lending fyftem, which they fuperadded to their other fources of income, it is not at all furprifing that, in length of time, they fhould have accumulated much pecuniary wealth, the precarioufnefs of which however will not impofe upon the real political Economift. During the laft century the Dutch made fuch a rapid progrefs towards opulence, that their artificial fyftem was regarded by political writers of that age, of no fmall difcernment, as far preferable for fecuring the profperity of nations, to the poffeffion of an extenfive and well cultivated territory. Among thofe who were dazzled and mifled by the profperity of the Dutch were Sir William Temple and Sir William Petty, the latter of whom not perceiving upon what a weak and infecure foundation that profperity refted, went fo far as to wifh it to be a model for England, faying that England would be more rich and more powerful, if Scotland, Ireland, and Wales were funk in the fea, provided their inhabitants were firft transferred within the bounds of England. Such are the wild and dangerous conclufions that fenfible men are led into, when the true and fundamental principle of the wealth of nations is not attended to by them, and when in their plans of policy they fubftitute

the

the unstable and transient revenue arising from commerce, for the permanent and secure revenue arising from the cultivation of territory.

How widely different are the maxims of the American States from those of Sir William Petty! Were the Americans to adopt his commercial system of getting rich, they might all find room in the peninsula bounded by the Delaware and the Chesapeak, which, with very little labour, might be made a complete island; and there, bounded by the sea, they might direct their views to commerce and navigation, and by living penuriously might acquire, in progress of time, a monied capital. They have however wisely chosen to accumulate men rather than to accumulate ducats; and by giving their chief attention to the most valuable of all capitals, an extensive territory, and by the improvement of that capital, they have acquired more power and more wealth in four years than the Dutch acquired in an hundred years. The increase of population in the American States from the year 1790 to 1794, is found by a late census to be 1,321,364 persons, who estimated in a pecuniary light, at the price only of negroes, is an augmentation of national capital of near 100 millions sterling.

If the sources of opulence of the Dutch above enumerated (which, as we have seen, are not dependent upon manufactures, and which fascinated the politicians of the last century) are inferior, in point of abundance, to the source arising from the cultivation of an extensive, a fertile, and connected territory, they are no less inferior in point of stability. Their fishing trade does not now produce one-half of what it formerly produced, becaufe the Swedes, the Britons, the French, the Americans have all interfered in that branch of induftry. Their Eaft India monopoly of fpices is on the point of being terminated, becaufe the climates in the Weft will foon furnifh thofe fpices; and their carrying trade has alfo declined from the fame caufe that has occafioned the decline of their fifhing trade. Now fuppofing, what is but too likely, that thefe three fources of the opulence of the Dutch fhould ftill fuffer a greater wane, and likewife that their neighbours, to whom they at prefent ftand in the light of abfentees, fhould be wife enough to pay them back the money borrowed from them, they would foon have the fad experience that poverty and tenantlefs houfes would overfpread their whole country, notwithftanding their greateft fkill and greateft induftry in manufactures.

Are then manufactures of no value to a nation? Very far otherwife. What would man in his prefent ftate be, were he to be without houfes, without clothes, and without furniture. Thefe and a great variety of other kinds of manufactures, are, according to the prefent condition of men, juftly termed neceffaries of life; and confequently manufacturers are moft defervedly to be deemed a *neceffary clafs* in fociety. That however does not make them a *productive clafs*, that is, a clafs which renews the revenue of fociety, or gives any augmentation or increafe to that revenue. The manufacturer becaufe he produces fomething of value, has been moft erroneoufly fuppofed to augment the

mafs

mass of national opulence, to double or triple the value of what is put into his hands, and consequently to increase in the same proportion the income of society. Hardly is there any political or commercial writer who has not in some degree adopted this error; and among those who have been formerly thus misled, I must include myself. But close and frequent meditation on the subject has given me the clearest conviction that no augmentation of the revenue of society arises from the labour of a manufacturer, except in the case of its being sold abroad. In that case indeed the profit of the exporter becomes the profit of the nation where he lives. That nation however would, as has been before proved, be a greater gainer, were the labour of the cultivator to be exported rather than the labour of the manufacturer. The manufacturer, almost in all cases, produces something of value to society; but he produces that value only by the extinction of another value, previously provided for him by the cultivator. The merit of the manufacturer is, that he gives a fixed and permanent value to the more perishable riches procured by the cultivator, or rather bestowed by nature on the labour of the cultivator; but he does not augment that primary and sole source of riches. Thus the beef and bread furnished by the cultivator to certain masons and carpenters have given us Westminster Bridge. The beef and bread are gone, but the bridge we have in exchange. Thus the onions produced by the cultivators in Egypt, and expended by some manufacturers there, have given us one of the great pyramids.

mids. Thus the linen manufacturer, at the expence of the fubfiftence of his workmen, furnifhed by the cultivator, will turn the flax, furnifhed alfo by the cultivator, into a commodity which is tranfmitted by careful houfewives from one generation to another. Thus the leaves of one mulberry-tree will, through the intervention of fome filk-worms, yield perhaps a guinea's-worth of filk; but the increafe, or revenue, does not originate from the filk-worms, but from the mulberry-tree; that is, from the cultivator, affifted by the bounty of nature. The filk-worm, in this view, is the exact type of all manufacturers whatever. Having his fubfiftence furnifhed to him, he gives in return a permanent commodity, equal in value to that fubfiftence.

But do not we fee many manufacturers get rich? Yes, certainly: and this very circumftance of their acquiring a capital, has led political and commercial writers into the falfe conclufion, that manufacturers created a capital. In a profeffed enquiry into the nature and caufes of the Wealth of Nations, one would have expected to have found this error clearly refuted; but fo far otherwife, Dr. Smith has interwoven it into the whole of his performance, which renders that performance worfe than ufelefs as a political treatife, a mere caftle of cards, erected without a foundation, and affording no habitation for the politician. If a manufacturer gets rich, or, in Dr. Smith's phrafe, acquires a great capital by the profits of a manufacture, the refolution of fuch manufacture into its conftituent parts, will prove to every perfon open to conviction, that no manufacture

ture when fold at home, increafes the income of a nation, however it may add greatly to the conveniences of that nation. Whatever value is put upon any manufacture, it is refolvable into three other values; namely, the value of the raw material of which it is made, the value of the wages expended in its fabrication, and thirdly, the value or profit which the manufacturer fuperadds to the other two values, as a recompence to himfelf. Now none of thefe three values comprehends in it any increafe of general revenue, confequently the three together cannot form any increafe of general revenue. They only occafion a commutation or transfer of the revenue previoufly provided by the cultivator, by giving a permanency to that revenue under a new form. Nay, in fome cafes (which, indeed, rarely happen) they do not even do that; for we have inftances wherein the labour of the manufacturer is quite unprofitable both to himfelf and to fociety. Thus the editor of the pofthumous edition of Lord Bolingbroke's works, would have much better have been doing nothing, than employing himfelf in that publication, by which he loft feveral hundred pounds, becaufe the work did not fell. Thus the maker of a time-piece which nobody will buy, becaufe it is inaccurate, has actually produced nothing of value, though he may have employed feveral years in the conftruction of it. Thus the calico printer, who unluckily has ufed a pattern that fuits noboby's tafte, finds by the refult, that his labour has added no value to the calico. Such cafes, indeed are very rare; but they plainly prove, that a manufacturer only enriches himself by being a seller, and that when he ceases to be a seller, his profits are immediately at a stand, because they are not natural profits, but artificial. The cultivator, on the other hand (supposing a little domestic thrift), may exist, and thrive, and multiply, without selling any thing: consequently, a nation of cultivators may be a most prosperous nation without much exterior traffic.

In the same manner as an individual manufacturer gets rich, so a manufacturing district gets rich. It abounds in sellers, who draw profits to themselves from the revenues of those to whom they sell their manufactures. Were the populous manufacturing cities of Great Britain not to be great sellers (I mean within the limits of Great Britain), they would soon dwindle down to the size of moderate villages; but as by means of their riders and correspondents they disperse their fabrics through every corner of the island, they consequently concentre profits from every corner of the island to their own district. But all these profits, whatever their amount may be, are precisely so much deducted out of the profits of the buyers of those manufactures, consequently no national income, or augmentation of national revenue. Let it be farther observed, that one half of the nation do not supply their own wants. Now it is the great praise of manufacturers, that they supply their own wants; they return a full equivalent for their own subsistence, which is a most material point in their favour, and constitutes them one of the essential classes of society. The

returning

returning this equivalent for their subsistence, though it does not increase any revenue, yet, by rendering the revenue permanent, while half the nation are dissipating theirs without any return, must consequently fix ease and opulence in a manufacturing quarter in a greater degree than in a quarter where neither cultivation nor manual industry is much attended to. Suppose twenty-four poor females were to have their subsistence furnished to them; and twelve of those females, imitating the practice in Guernsey, should after dinner assemble alternately in each other's houses with their knitting-needles, and spend the evenings in conversation and knitting of stockings; while the twelve other females after dinner sit down to cards, and spend the evenings in play. These last, it is plain, would ever remain in indigence; but the former would in process of time have something to sell. Nevertheless, the value of what they offered to market would only be a retribution of the value of their subsistence, which by their industry they had fixed, while the card-players had dissipated theirs without any return. These twelve industrious females represent the whole class of manufacturers, who by yielding a return of a permanent nature, equal in value to the subsistence they consume, give, by this transformation, a certain stability to what was before of a more perishable nature. Thus a cart-load of manufactured cloth may be equivalent to five cart-loads of corn, because it has cost five cart-loads of corn to pay for the wool and for the wages of the workmen. An additional value it cannot produce,

without

without drawing that additional value from fome other revenue before created, and therefore yields no increafe. But ftill it is a circumftance extremely in favour of manufacturers, that they do not, like half the nation, eat their bread for nothing, or for an old fong; but give in return what all nations both civilized and uncivilized have ever deemed neceffary not only to their well being, but to their very being; confequently manufacturers have a moft juft right to be called an effential clafs in fociety, next after the cultivators. Add to the above, that working manufacturers in towns and villages being accuftomed to confider the value of time, are often led to employ their fpare hours in cultivating a potatoe fpot, or a fmall garden, which is a labour that yields an increafe; and in the populous towns the rich manufacturers, inftead of a large eftablifhment of fervants, hounds, and horfes, difpofe of their furplus wealth in building and ornamenting villas, or improving of farms, which places them in the productive clafs of cultivators, and confequently adds to the wealth of their diftrict. Laftly, though manufacturers, by their labour, do not increafe the revenue or income of a ftate, yet the demand for their fubfiftence encourages the farmers in their neighbourhood to produce that fubfiftence, confequently the lands in fuch fituations are generally better cultivated than they would otherwife be; and this better cultivation, adds both to the wealth of the diftrict, and the wealth of the nation. All thefe confiderations united ferve to explain how wealth and opulence may be concentered

tered in a manufacturing diſtrict, and how maſter manufacturers may acquire great capitals, though, at the ſame time, manufacturers themſelves do neither originate nor increaſe the income of a nation.

As manufacturers, however, in general, prevent that part of the national income which goes to their ſubſiſtence from being diſſipated, but return it in ſome vendible fabrick, that may be either uſed or ſold, it will be a great object with every wiſe ſtateſman to give every encouragement to increaſe the number of manufacturers, at the expence of ſuch other claſſes in ſociety as are by no means eſſential claſſes. A nation cannot give too much into manufactures, provided it draws its manufacturers from the ſupernumeraries in other claſſes, whoſe ſubſiſtence is in reality a tax upon ſociety. Every one acknowledges that the indigent poor at preſent on the pariſh rolls in Great Britain, who may perhaps exceed 400,000 in number, and who contribute nothing to their own ſubſiſtence, are a tax and burthen upon ſociety; and in ſo far as they are really helpleſs, their ſubſiſtence is a moſt neceſſary and a moſt humane tax. But were one-fourth of their number, or 100,000 of them, to be found capable of manual labour, the eſtabliſhing ſuch regulations as would transfer that fourth into the claſs of manufacturers, would probably ſave a million annually to the nation. The manufacturing claſs in Great Britain might alſo be profitably reinforced from the ſupernumerary and uſeleſs individuals in many other claſſes of ſociety. Were the many ſupernumerary thouſands that could be ſpared from among

among retailing shop-keepers, from among ale-house-keepers, inn-keepers, apothecaries, attornies, menial servants, &c. &c. who are now a much heavier tax upon society than the parochial poor, to be transferred into the class of manufacturers, we should soon find manufactures more abundant, and at much cheaper prices; that is, the prosperity of the nation would be thereby greatly increased, because probably half a million of people, who at present are subsisted by the community, without returning to it any equivalent, would in that case return the full value of their subsistence.

A nation, however, would be extremely blind to its own interests, who should augment the class of manufacturers at the expence of the class of cultivators. That would be, in a manner, to neglect the working of a rich gold mine, for the sake of working a silver mine, that did no more than pay the wages of the workmen. The labour of the manufacturer, we have seen, is profitable in so far as it returns the value of his subsistence; but the labour of the cultivator not only returns the value of his own subsistence, but, when skilfully applied, and aided by the bounty of nature, yields a surplus sufficient to feed four or five other persons; consequently the more numerous the class of skilful cultivators is in any nation, and the greater the fertility of its soil, the greater will be the resources of that nation. It is the mass of surplusses occasioned by the whole of the cultivators, that forms the revenue of every other class in society. It is that which sets the carpenter and mason to work; it is that which pays

pays the foldier and failor; it is that which enriches the fhop-keeper; it is that which pays the fees of the lawyer and phyfician. In fhort, the only fource of every payment in a ftate is the produce of its lands and its feas, exclufive of the fmall income it may acquire by foreign commerce, fmall in comparifon of the immenfity of the other, and often impolitically procured at the expence of that other. What clafs in fociety fo much claims the encouragement and fupport of a wife legiflature as that clafs, which alone originates and increafes the wealth of fociety, by furnifhing a furplus much beyond its own fubfiftence. Thirty hay-makers will in five or fix days make an hundred pounds worth of hay; a value exceeding their own fubfiftence five or fix fold. Twenty negroes in Carolina will produce as much rice as will purchafe the labour of an hundred manufacturers in Great Britain. The patriarch Ifaac, we are told, fowed and reaped an hundred fold, which, allowing even one-half for expence, leaves a neat profit of 5000 per cent. The cultivators of rice in China, it is faid, often reap an hundred fold, and have two crops in one year; which, fuppofing the fame degree of expence as before, will give a neat profit of 10,000 per cent. But were the profit of the cultivator, as in lefs fertile climates, to amount only to 400 per cent, or even to 100 per cent; or even but to 50 per cent, it has this advantage over the profits of every other clafs in fociety *that it is all increafe*, not being formed by the diminution of the revenue of any other clafs. Nature yields the profit to him, and through

through him, to the whole community, who have nothing else to subsist upon, excepting perhaps, as above-mentioned, some small gains from foreign commerce; which commerce, however, would soon cease to exist, if it were not for the support of the cultivator.

Since, then, the class of cultivators is that alone which originates and increases the revenue of a state, a wise nation will zealously pursue every measure that may tend to increase the numbers in that class, not only from the many unessential classes in society, but even from the class of manufacturers itself. Instead of making manufactures the attractive principle of cultivation, such a nation will follow the much more natural and more profitable system of making cultivation the attractive principle of manufactures. While there is in any corner of its territory lands unimproved, it will advance its prosperity much more rapidly, and establish it much more solidly, by directing the industry of its inhabitants, not to manufactures, but to the cultivation of those lands. The labour of the manufacturer we have seen is sterile or unfruitful in comparison of that of the cultivator. This last, by originating subsistence, originates and supports population; and by originating more than his own subsistence, creates annually a new fund for purchasing all the conveniencies that it is in the power of the manufacturer to produce, whether that manufacturer resides in his own parish or ten thousand miles off, provided the communication, or mutual intercourse between them, be unobstructed.

From

From not investigating in what the Wealth of Nations consists, and where it originates, the want of manufactures has been by many writers alleged as an apology for neglected and deficient agriculture. The great cry has been, even among legislators themselves, let us have but manufactures, and then we shall have well-cultivated lands. The false principle of Dr. Smith, that manufactures produce a revenue, has given support to this very misleading and pernicious doctrine—a doctrine, indeed, of much older date than that of Dr. Smith's Enquiry. It is, however, with great pleasure I observe, that several of the authors of the statistical account of Scotland, particularly the Rev. Mr. Oliver, in the judicious account of his parish of Corstorphine, view the subject in a very different light. Like faithful pastors, as well as skilful politicians, they plainly shew, by many judicious arguments, that from motives of religion and morality, as well as from motives of worldly advantage, the cultivation of the territory ought to have the preference to the establishment of manufactures, more especially as manufactures are at present established in many parts of Great Britain. Agriculture, I hope, will soon be viewed by the whole British nation, and by the whole Irish nation, in the same light as it is viewed by those reverend writers; and that it should be so viewed, is the great purpose of my present discourse.

If no national revenue proceeds from manufactures, and if all national revenue proceeds from agriculture, which truths I presume the preceding pages have made very manifest, it may then, I think

think, be expected, that the land owners in both iſlands, zealouſly concurring with their reſpective legiſlatures, will without delay adopt ſuch meaſures as may ſpread cultivation over every mountain and over every valley in Great Britain and Ireland. While a field admitting cultivation can be found for every idler, let no idler be without a field. Houſes of induſtry are good things; but fields of induſtry are much better; and were Great Britain and Ireland to be wholly overſpread with ſuch fields, the annual revenue of theſe iſlands would thereby ſoon acquire a real augmentation of twenty millions ſterling. I ſay a real augmentation, and not a nominal. A nominal augmentation only ſerves to heighten prices, to the prejudice of foreign commerce; but a real augmentation would actually lower them, and increaſe both the numbers and the eaſe of the people.

Great Britain and Ireland have the means of this augmentation within themſelves. It may be effected without treaties of commerce; without any acquiſition of new territory, and without any increaſe of the balance of trade. But it cannot be effected unleſs the poſſeſſors of land give every encouragement to thoſe who are willing to undergo the fatigue of cultivating them. From the falſe notion that manufactures are a ſource of wealth, land owners are extremely ready to give perpetual leaſes to manufacturers. But what an overflow of wealth would they not procure to themſelves, and to the nation, would they but ſhew an equal readineſs to give perpetual leaſes to cultivators, from whoſe

labours

labours it has been shewn, and not from the labours of manufacturers, the Wealth of Nations originates.

Let cultivators have the same security given to them that is lavished upon manufacturers, and thousands and ten thousands would quickly appear as ready to contract an alliance with their native soil, as the vine is to contract an alliance with the lofty poplar. We should then hear of hundreds of thousands of new marriages between farmers and their farms, no matter whether of great or of small extent, for what is great to the capacity and means of one farmer, may be small to the capacity and means of another. The giving security to the labourer would give activity to the spade and the plough, on every waste and on every heath in Great Britain. Innumerable buildings would be raised by new cultivators, not only along our rivers, our canals, and public roads; but in sequestered places, now inhabited by moor fowl and wild deer. And intermixed with the buildings of those new cultivators, would be the houses of new manufacturers; so that a traveller journeying from south to north, or from east to west, would find every where over the whole island, a neat habitation within a mile, or within half a mile of another.

A decided preference to cultivation, by no means implies a neglect of manufactures. On the contrary, like natural genius assisted by erudition, *conjurant amice;* they in most cases mutually promote each others prosperity; and would more especially do so, if manufacturers, instead of being impolitically crowded together in great towns, were every where

where intermixed with the cultivators. By this fyftem the unprofitable wafte of expence in tranfporting goods forwards and backwards would be avoided. Manufacturers would every where be near to their fubfiftence; and cultivators would no where be obliged to go far from their habitations for the common fabrics they wanted to purchafe. Above all a virtuous fimplicity of manners would be preferved among the people; and while induftry and content would be every where diffufed, the land would overflow literally with milk and honey, and the population, the wealth and power of the ftate refting on their natural foundation, would gradually rife to the utmoft degree of profperity that the ifland was fufceptible of. Such would be the happy confequences of adopting the fyftem of the Economifts, in confidering the produce of the foil as the fource of all revenue, and giving the preference to that branch of induftry, which has for its object the augmentation of that produce.

Having, I think, clearly proved that the revenue of a ftate arifes folely from the produce of its lands, and that Dr. Smith's arguments in fupport of the productivenefs of manufactures are altogether illufive, I fhall now proceed to confider the fundamental error of the French Economifts in ranking the proprietors of lands as a productive clafs in fociety; and fhall explain the principle founded in nature, which when acted upon, renders the proprietors of land, not indeed a productive clafs, but an *effential clafs*, and the moft honourable clafs in fociety.

In so far as a proprietor of land cultivates his own possession, or a part of his own possession, he certainly ranks among cultivators, and consequently is one in the productive class in society. But when he does not actually interfere with the cultivation of his land, and merely lets it out to be cultivated by others for a certain rent, (which in Europe is the case with ninety-nine proprietors in an hundred) it is evident he from that moment ceases to be of the productive class, and becomes one in the many unproductive classes of the community.

Every class of men in a state, except the class of cultivators, is properly an unproductive class. But among the indefinite number of unproductive classes some are essential to the being of a state, while others are wholly unessential, though they may be convenient for its well being. What is essential to the being of a thing, is that without which the thing itself could not exist. Thus it is essential to gold to be incorruptible, to be yellow, to be very weighty, very mallable, &c. but it is not essential to gold to be round or square. To a globe or circle it is essential to be round. To a musket it seems essential to have a barrel, a lock, a stock, and a ramrod; but it is not essential to it to have inlaid work or gold or silver ornaments. Thus in examining the classes in civil society that are essential to its very existence, we shall find that they may be all reduced to the four following; first of all the productive class of cultivators; secondly, the class of manufacturers; thirdly, the class of defenders; and fourthly, the

the clafs of inftructors; for every civil fociety muft be fed, muft be clothed, defended, and inftructed.

On the fuppofition of the Abbé de St. Pierre of *une paix perpetuelle*, or a perpetual peace, the clafs of defenders would ceafe to be an effential clafs in fociety; and in a ftate that chofe to be as illiterate as the Romans were before they became acquainted with Grecian literature, or as the Grecians themfelves were till long after the Trojan war, the clafs of inftructors would alfo ceafe to be an effential clafs. But as the corrupt nature of man renders defence abfolutely neceffary; and as his mental improvement ought no lefs to be an object with him than his corporeal conveniences and enjoyments, the claffes of defenders and inftructors are as juftly entitled to be deemed effential as the claffes of cultivators and manufacturers, and I have therefore mentioned them as fuch, though the clafs of cultivators be the only productive clafs.

The proprietors of land as mere receivers of land rents are not an effential clafs in fociety, any more than engravers, ftatuaries, &c. It is by the conftitutional appropriation of the rents of land to the defence of the ftate, that the receivers of thofe rents become an effential clafs in fociety. By feparating the rents of lands from the conftitutional purpofe of the defence of the ftate, the receivers of thofe rents inftead of being an effential clafs, render themfelves one of the moft uneffential and moft burdenfome claffes in fociety. This fundamental maxim is applicable to all ftates; but I fhall confider it chiefly in regard to Great Britain. In Great Britain the
rents

rents of the lands may be stated at twenty-five millions, making a burden upon agriculture amounting to one third, and in some cases to near one half of all that the island produces, which, as has been shewn, is our only revenue.

The cultivation of the ground is absolutely necessary for the subsistence of man, but the payment of a rent is not absolutely necessary for the cultivation of the ground. The farmer could cultivate it as well without paying a tax of fifty per cent, or thirty per cent for leave to cultivate it; and we have the experience before our eyes, that young states thrive exceedingly, by being exempt from that unnecessary tax. What has drawn so many settlers from Europe over to the late British Colonies in America, but the happy circumstance of having lands without paying any rent, and formerly with the impolitic indulgence of paying hardly any public burdens. The circumstance of paying no rent has been the attracting loadstone to thousands and ten thousands to the American shores. Now can it be said that the lands of America yield the less, because the cultivators of them are also the possessors? Certainly not. On the contrary, the cultivators of the lands in America being at the same time the possessors of those lands, are thereby exempted from a tax of 33 per cent, which the cultivators in Great Britain and Ireland are subject to, which circumstance has been the very animating soul of the agriculture of the Americans, enabling them, in the commerce of grain, to undersel their mother country in foreign markets. Nay, it has even

even ferved them as a bounty of thirty-three per cent, to pour their corn in upon us, which was the fame thing in point of policy on our fide, as if a duty of thirty-three per cent had been impofed upon Newcaftle coals, and American coals had been admitted duty free.

If the practical example of the late Britifh American Colonies proves to a demonftration, that ftates may not only exift, but flourifh with the greateft profperity, without paying any rents for the lands that yield them their fubfiftence, the plain conclufion is, that land rents abftractedly confidered are unneceffary burdens, and that land renters in that fenfe are not an effential clafs in fociety.

How then will a wife government, acting in conformity to the principles of nature, render the receivers of land rents an effential clafs in fociety? The political Economift anfwers by affigning them an appropriate occupation; for it is contrary to all reafon, and to all policy, to allow mere idlers in a ftate, or to fuffer thofe who receive one third, or even but one fourth of the whole income of the kingdom, to do nothing for it in return. We are by the law of our nature condemned to earn our bread by the fweat of our brow; but no law can juftly exift, by which one man fhall earn his bread by the fweat of another man's brow, without rendering for it fome equivalent.

The fum of twenty-five millions fterling, making between one third, and one fourth of the whole income of Great Britain, being paid by the cultivators to the proprietors of land, and being, as appears, an

actual

actual burden upon the community, reafon and found policy point it out as the natural fund for the defence of the community. When thus applied by the legiflature, the poffeffors of thofe rents inftantly become not only an effential clafs in fociety; but an honourable clafs likewife; for honour will ever be freely allowed to thofe, whofe profeffion it is to be ready to rifk their lives in the defence of the community.

A cafe of danger to this kingdom, can hardly be fuppofed, that would require the military exertions of every fourth perfon in it, that is, that would abforb the fourth part of its yearly income, or in other words, the whole of the land rents. A part of thofe rents therefore may, without the rifk of any deficiency in point of defence, be appropriated to the annual maintenance of the fourth effential clafs in fociety, namely, the effential and honourable clafs of inftructors.

A full fourth, or, perhaps, near a third of the annual national income being thus applied, or applicable to the fupport of the defenders and inftructors, the people ought to be exempted from every fpecies of taxation for the purpofes of defence and inftruction, that is, government ought to draw the whole of the national fupplies in all cafes, from the rents of lands, as thofe rents afford an ample fund for every fuppofed cafe of emergency.

Such is the natural confequence of the principles of the political Economifts, in refpect to countries where the cultivators pay rents for the lands they cultivate; and in thofe countries where the cultivators pay no rents for the lands they occupy, but are the masters of their own surpluses, the defence of their lands, in case of an attack from an enemy, must come out of those surpluses, or what is worse, must come out of the capital possession itself, upon the principle that half a loaf is better than no bread.

Those whose minds have been preoccupied with the expediency and rectitude of the present most chaotic system of taxation, and with the notion of the vast income arising to the state from manufactures, have expressed great surprize and astonishment at the conclusion of the Economists, that the public supplies ought to be drawn wholly and directly from the rents of lands, or from the surplus produce of lands, that is, that there should be no tax but a land tax. To the superficial it has been matter of drollery; to the serious a stumbling block; and to the half-knowing an inexplicable riddle. In France, Germany, and Holland, it has had a great variety of opposers, as well as of approvers. The witty Voltaire attacked it in one of his most flimsy productions, L'homme a Quarante Ecus. The serious Necker expresses his doubts of it; and argues upon its impracticability; but his arguments are such as most clearly prove, that the subject had not been justly conceived by him.

In Britain, Dr. Adam Smith views it askance, and cautiously shoves off the discussion of its merits, in the following evasive words. ' Without entering,
' he says, into the disagreeable discussion of the
' metaphysical arguments, by which the Economists
' support

' support their very ingenious theory, it will suf-
' ficiently appear from the following review what
' are the taxes that fall finally on the rent of land,
' and what are those that fall finally upon some
' other fund.' The perusal and reperusal of that
very long and desultory review, to which he refers,
has not to me discovered that difference of funds,
from whence taxes originate, which he was to make
so evident. The Economists found their system of
policy and finance upon the three principles of
number, weight, and *measure*; and if we are to
reckon with Dr. Smith, *number, weight,* and *measure,* to be metaphysics, I should be glad to know
what we are to consider as physics.

Though Dr. Smith thus glides over in a most
cursorily manner, a subject of enquiry of the greatest
importance to the Wealth of Nations; yet another
British political writer, Mr. Arthur Young, thinks it
deserving of a very particular discussion. Mr.
Young declares himself a warm antagonist to the
idea of the Economists, of drawing the whole of the
public supplies from the rents of lands, or from the
surplus produce of land, and endeavours to combat
it by fair reasoning; but reasoning that is not substantial. Great Britain and Ireland are much indebted to him, for the persevering and patriotic
zeal with which he has illustrated and enforced
many truths, important to their prosperity. He
every where appears to me a candid searcher after
truth, disclaiming any hypothesis, though inadver-
tently adopted by himself, that has not truth for its
basis. Therefore in giving a full refutation to his

very

very erroneous doctrines on this point, and others connected with it, and dependent upon it, I doubt not but he will think me entitled to his warmest thanks. My appeal shall be from Mr. Young ill informed, to Mr. Young better informed, and I flatter myself that I shall have him among the first and most zealous of my proselytes.

Having in the preceding pages explained the fundamental principle of the Economists, namely, that a state possessing a large territory has no other revenue than that arising from the produce of its lands, (exclusive of some small income from foreign commerce) and as one third of that produce is in Great Britain given by those who raise it, to a class of men, who if they were not to defend the state, would in a political sense have nothing to do, the defence of the state therefore naturally and politically devolves upon that class of men, as every other class of men in a state has its respective employment. From the fundamental principle above mentioned and above explained, it follows, that since there ought to be no other tax for the defence of the state than a land tax, that tax ought to be most carefully collected, in a just proportion according to the exigencies of the state, and that it is highly criminal in any receiver of land rents, to withhold from Government his due proportion of those rents.

A crowd of new ideas, in regard to finance, will immediately succeed in the minds of those who are fully convinced of the truth of the preceding principle, and its corollary; and their eyes will be opened to the insignificance of almost all that Hume, Montes-

Montesquieu, Neckar, Dr. Smith, and many others have said upon the subject. The wild deviation from the true principle of taxation, which is now, and for near two hundred years has been, the practice of every European state, has served as an unsurmountable barrier to the acumen and spirit of enquiry of those writers. They have shewn themselves as little acquainted with the nature of public supply and national defence, as we were with New Holland before the discoveries of Captain Cook. Among the few nothings mentioned by Montesquieu on the subject of taxation, he most decidedly, but absurdly says, the *natural* tax of moderate governments is the duty laid on merchandize, which is really paid by the consumer. Wonderful! we have not however one word from him, why such a tax is more natural than a tax upon dogs, or upon hackney coaches. The complaints of the excess of taxes in France, had made an impression upon him; and he makes the following remark upon that subject in general, which greatly supports the system of the Economists, and might have opened to him the right tract, if his mind had not been completely hood-winked as to that point. ' It was the excess
' of taxes, he says, that occasioned the prodigious
' facility, with which the Mahomedans carried on
' their conquests. Instead of a continual series of
' extortions devised by the subtle avarice of the
' Greek Emperors, the people were subjected to a
' *single tribute,* which was paid and collected with
' ease. Thus they were far happier in obeying a
' barbarous nation, than a corrupt government, in
' which

' which they suffered every inconvenience of loft
' liberty, with all the horrors of prefent flavery.'
This *fingle tribute*, paid with eafe by the Greeks to the conquering Turks, was probably the produce of the foil at prime coft, that is, unenhanced by nominal money, by excifes, &c. The plain underftandings of the Turks pointed out to them that the produce of the foil was the natural fource of income, and that it was true policy to apply to that fource directly, and to ufe every means to make it more abundant. And that fyftem they feem, through fucceeding ages, to have perfevered in; for the eleganr Bufbequius, the Imperial ambaffador, in his letters from Turkey, written near two hundred years ago, mentions with admiration the great fertility and well-cultivated fields of Afia Minor; and we have it alfo upon good authority, that not half a century ago the bufhel of wheat was fold at Smyrna for lefs than feventeen-pence*.

Mr. Young, in his treatife entitled *Political Arithmetic*, oppofes with much zeal the idea of a fingle tribute, or, in other words, a land-tax, adequate to the defence of the ftate in every emergency; but his arguments, when examined upon the principles of the Economifts, will be found to be mere delufions, though of a very dangerous tendency to the public welfare, while they remain unrefuted. It would be a very tedious bufinefs to expofe all the errors in that performance, which are thick fcattered in the midft of many ufeful truths;

* Vide Tracts on the Corn Trade, p. 33.

and

and it would likewife be an unneceffary tafk, as the refutation of the effential errors will lead to the detection of the others, and take from the whole the power of further mifleading.

It is an idea of Mr. Young, and of many others befides him, that near one-half of the income of the nation arifes from manufactures; and upon this idea he fays, page 239, ' The income of our foil ' is very confiderable, but does not make much ' above half the total income of the ftate. The ' profits and labour in commerce, manufactures, and ' arts, are of a vaft amount, confequently to ex- ' empt them all from taxation, and throw the ' whole burden on land, would be unequal and op- ' preffive in the higheft degree.' This reafoning would be juft, were any revenue in reality to arife to the ftate from manufactures made and fold at home; but as I have above fhewn in my remarks on Dr. Smith's fifth obfervation, that manufactures, though greatly beneficial to the community, really produce no revenue, that is, no actual augmentation or renovation of wealth, it confequently follows, that no public fupply can be drawn from them. There is not, therefore, the fmalleft neceffity for further enlarging on this poin·, as what is before faid is a fufficient explanation of it.

I fhall proceed to confider another fundamental error of Mr. Young, which pervades the whole of his performance. He has, like Dr. Adam Smith, never once confidered the political nature of rent paid by a cultivator for leave to cultivate the ground.

ground. With him the rent of land is something sacred, indefeasibly appropriated to the landlords, who have a right to increase it as much as possible, and to dispose of it as they please. It is no burden upon the cultivators, that is, upon the community at large; for the cultivators, he says, in this country, feel very little the burden of taxation, which he attempts to prove by several cursory observations on the excises, customs, window-lights, poor rates, and other taxes, totally overlooking the payment of rent, that is, the payment of six shillings and eight pence in the pound, or even but five shillings in the pound, by the farmer, of all his earnings and profits. Sentiments somewhat similar I remember to have read several years ago, apologising for the conduct of some land owners in the Highlands of Scotland, who stating that they had a right to do as they pleased with their own, upon that principle raised their rents exorbitantly, and thereby compelled their tenants to emigrate to America. The tenants practically replied to this false principle of their unfeeling landlords, by shewing them that they had a right to inhabit where they pleased. Now, according to the principle of the Economists, every man in a state ought to have some occupation; and the rents of lands being a surplus income falling into the lap of the land owners, without their contributing to the production of that surplus, and tending to enhance the price of things one-third or one-fourth, reason requires that the land owners should do something for the community in return for the privilege of having this surplus secured

to

to them by the community. The words of Cicero to this purpose are very apposite, 'Major hereditas venit unicuique vestrum in iisdem bonis a jure & a legibus, quam ab iis, a quibus illa ipsa bona relicta sunt;' that is, You are not so much indebted to your rich father or rich grand-father for the great landed income you possess, as to the laws and government which protect you in the possession of that income. Government having thus a natural claim upon those whom it protects in the enjoyment of great incomes, to the production of which they contribute no labour of their own, has a right to ask for a part of this surplus for the defence of the state, as being the only disposable revenue in the state. For the cultivator, it is evident, cannot both fight and at the same time provide subsistence for the community; the fisherman when fishing cannot be fighting; the manufacturer, if any thing be taken from his wages, must either starve or raise his wages, which last tends to load commodities with an artificial value. The state, however, must be defended; and thus, by placing the defence upon the surplus revenue, every landlord in the kingdom becomes politically as much a tenant to the state, as any of his farmers is a tenant to him.

Another very capital error which Mr. Young endeavours to establish is, that an equal land tax raised in proportion to the value of the rents, would be a most pernicious system. His short argument in support of this error is, that the improver would thereby be taxed according to his improvements. Now if we examine this herculean

argu-

argument, printed by him in capital letters, we shall find that it is wholly unsubstantial, and that Mr. Young himself will assist us in refuting his own false doctrine. In the first place, his conclusion does not follow from his premises; for a real four shillings in the pound, though not now paid, may be demanded from lands that have received no improvement for these hundred years. But waving this oversight, the Economist affirms, that the argument of Mr. Young against a valuation of the land tax according to the real amount of the rents, is the strongest argument in favour of such a valuation. When does a creditor most naturally look for the payment of a debt, but when his debtor is in cash? When ought government so properly to ask more of a landlord, as when that landlord asks more of his tenant? Does not a landlord who raises his rent upon a new lease, tax the improver according to his improvement? Does he not, in effect, argue to the following purpose with his farmer—Your farm twenty years ago was worth only 50l. a year, but in consequence of your good management it is now worth 70l. a year; therefore I shall require that rent from you during the present lease. Every one will readily acknowledge that within this half-century the rents of lands are risen very considerably over the whole island. What can this rise be owing to but to real improvement, or the presumption of future improvement. If upon the presumption of future improvement, which I am afraid is too often the case, then the improver is not taxed in proportion to the improvement he

has

has made; which is juft and equitable, becaufe the property is really become more valuable; but according to an improvement *in futuro*, which may never take place at all, confequently he may be forced to pay a new taxation without any new fund to fupport that taxation. But hear what may be concluded from Mr. Young himfelf. From his information, the rents in Norfolk are now four times higher than they were forty years ago, and the tenants in that county are in a very thriving ftate. It may be prefumed, that this fourfold rife of rent in Norfolk is founded upon improvement of fome kind or other; for to found it upon no improvement would not be juft and equitable. If, then, improvement has enabled the land owners in Norfolk to quadruple their rents within the fpace of forty years, and at the fame time to enrich their tenants, it plainly follows, that to tax the improver in proportion to his improvements, has not been a pernicious fyftem in the county of Norfolk, and therefore would not be a pernicious fyftem if extended to the whole kingdom. Government, it muft ever be kept in mind, in requiring a land tax in proportion to the real value of the rents, is only the fecondary taxer; for the land owner precedes in raifing his rent according to the improvements made by his tenant; if, therefore, the land owner, who is the primary taxer, has acted equitably and judicioufly in demanding a higher rent, in confequence of a real improvement of the foil, government cannot act wrong in demanding the ufual proportion upon that new rent.—That is to fay, *An equal land*

land tax, raised in proportion to the real value of the rents, is a just and truly politic system.

A fourth erroneous doctrine, fondly embraced by Mr. Young, is the importance of high price to the prosperity of agriculture, and even to the prosperity of the nation. But this doctrine, inculcated by him in a variety of places, he leaves unsupported by any solid argument. It is, indeed, an excellent doctrine for those who could possess an exclusive monopoly of selling, and were never to be buyers; but as no class of men in a community, nor indeed any nation upon earth, can possess such a monopoly; and as all buyers run naturally to the cheap market, it is the heighth of political imprudence in a nation wishing to extend its foreign commerce, to give an artificial rise to prices by a needless augmentation of their pecuniary value. Will a bushel of wheat feed more people when sold for ten shillings than when sold for half-a-crown? Will a pound of gunpowder send a ball farther if sold for five shillings instead of one shilling? Similar questions may be extended to the whole circle of commerce, both internal and external, which would plainly prove that high price is not favourable to the extension either of manufacture or of agriculture.

Already it is affirmed that high price has deprived us of one branch of manufacture, the printing of English books for foreign sale, such books being now printed in France for the American market; and if high price be in like manner annexed to the productions of the plough, we shall thereby assuredly

edly be deprived of the profitable trade of the exportation of corn.

Were we to have no connection at all with foreign nations, high price or low price in all our internal dealings, suppoſing thoſe prices fixed and ſtable, would not affect our national proſperity, as the price of the ſubſiſtence of the labourer would ſtill regulate all other prices. In the one caſe, high price would permanently meet high price, as in the other, low price would permanently meet low price. But while that claſs in ſociety, from whom the revenue originates, are from year to year puſhing the nominal value of that revenue higher and higher, the balance between ſellers and buyers is kept in perpetual uncertainty, and the peaceful order of ſociety is thereby greatly diſturbed. Thoſe whoſe yearly ſalaries were adequate to their yearly wants, find that they have only a full ſupply for nine months; and thoſe whoſe weekly wages were adequate to ſeven days ſupply, find that they have only a full ſubſiſtence for four days, and to make them hold out, they muſt go upon ſhort allowance during the whole week. As this augmentation of the nominal value of the produce of land conſequently augments the nominal value of every thing elſe, the reſult is, that the landed gentleman is not thereby enriched, nor are ſellers in general enriched by it, ſince what they gain as ſellers, they preciſely expend in quality of buyers. Thus George Faulkener having occaſion to expend but little, probably gained as much by his Dublin Journal when ſold

for

for a farthing, as many of thofe who in London now fell their newfpaper for eighteen farthings; and he furnifhed for his farthing as many advertifements and as much news as they do for their eighteen farthings.

Another inftance of the unavailing power of high price to make rich, may be gathered from what was lately declared in the Houfe of Commons by Mr. Whitbread. Mr. Young, in his Political Arithmetic, gave it as a fign of national profperity, that the land rents of Norfolk had within forty years encreafed four-fold, not diftinguifhing what was nominal and what was real in that increafe, and now by Mr. Whitbread we are informed, that the Norfolk Barley, though not of a very good kind, is fo extravagantly dear, that brewers can hardly afford to purchafe it; that barley in general is fo high priced, that they have been obliged to brew porter of an inferior quality, and are doubtful whether they fhall be able to continue the trade.

The trade, however, might be continued without lofs to the brewer, were the price of porter and other malt liquor to be doubled, were falaries and wages to be doubled, and the price of home manufactures to be doubled. But in what refpect would the nation be a gainer by thefe new nominal values, taking into view either its connection with foreign ftates, or confidering it independantly of any relation to thofe ftates. In the former cafe it would infallibly oblige our foreign cuftomers to leave off trading with us; and in the latter, fuppofing us not to be in need of foreign trade, it would only

make

make us pay with shillings what we now pay with sixpences.

There are few people, I believe, that would not confess that this duplication of prices, instead of being beneficial to the nation, would not be extremely prejudicial to it. Nevertheless, from the prevalence of a false principle in regard to taxation and the national utility of high price, we are most improvidently hastening towards it, by raising year after year, without necessity, the prices of the necessaries of life, and, as a corrective to that malady, forming plans for raising proportionally the rate of wages and the hire of labourers. True policy would rather recommend to keep wages and the hire of labourers steadily at their present rate, or at the rates at which they were forty years ago, and at the same time to use such means as to bring the necessary articles of living to correspond to those rates. If such had been our policy, national abundance with us would have been greater and more general, and volumes of laborious and patriotic disquisitions about meliorating the present state of labourers would have been rendered altogether unnecessary.

In a well-governed state, the price of labour may remain nearly unalterable for many centuries; and in the East Indies, before European modes of taxation were there introduced, the prices of things, it may be presumed, had remained nearly stationary for 2000 years. What more can the successive generations of men require, during their temporary life here, than to have fulness of bread; and, supposing pofing the population of one age equal to that of another, the fertility and cultivation of the ground the fame, and the medium of circulation not augmented or diminifhed, each fucceeding race of men may have that fulnefs of bread in the fame degree as the preceding, and at the fame price.

Were the permanent augmentation of the quantity of gold and filver to be alleged as a reafon for the rife in the prices of things, it will on that ground perhaps be found, that prices ought to be very little higher now than they were an hundred years ago; for fuppofing the quantity of fpecie to be doubled in this ifland fince the revolution, which may juftly be doubted, that ought not to double the prices; for if population in that time be increafed, fuppofe in the proportion of two to three, fifteen millions of coin would not now be a greater abundance of money than ten millions were at the revolution; confequently, if the quantity of circulating money was at the revolution ten millions, the nation ought now to poffefs confiderably more than thirty millions in fpecie, to occafion the prices of things to be twice as high as they were then; for, fince the revolution, the great improvements in the cultivation of the lands of the kingdom would otherwife have lowered prices, inftead of raifing them.

Though the real augmentation of the quantity of gold and filver affords no ground for the rife of prices, yet the moft extravagant augmentation of the expletive medium of circulation called paper-money (often the reprefentative of nothing) has

con-

contributed to overspread the land with high price in every direction, all ranks being now reciprocally complainers or complained of. As the great augmentation of this imaginary wealth has been a principal cause of introducing this epidemical malady into the kingdom, the true remedy for the illness will be found in removing that cause of it; namely, in suppressing this inefficient wealth, and studying without delay to augment the substantial wealth of the country by means of the plough. To the disgrace of our policy, it may lately have been said of us, Nummis Chartaceis locuples eget panis Britannorum gens; Britons, though wanting bread, abound in paper riches. The legislature that will sedulously endeavour to increase the physical wealth of the country, by encouraging the cultivation of its lands, may, without hesitation, say to every one of the coiners of imaginary money, Tolle tuas precor imagines et cum tota farragine migra; take yourself and your imaginary riches out of the country: it is substantial riches that are wanted; and this our lands will furnish us abundantly and cheaply, if you will but withdraw your interference. So far, however, from withdrawing their interference, they have lately most insidiously preached up the necessity of augmenting the present medium of circulation, and a newly-established bank in Norfolk-street upon that principle offers its services to the public. If a spirit of re-action do not occupy the country gentlemen, there is no knowing how far the mischief may lead. They, however, have a good precedent and example in the gentlemen

men of Brecknockshire; who, four or five years ago, in a county meeting, came to the refolution of not accepting in payments any notes of country banks. This example ought to be followed by every land owner in Great Britain; and the moment that peace returns, the land proprietors throughout the kingdom ought to declare to their tenants, that, except when the rent is to be paid in kind, they will not receive in payment of it any thing but gold and filver.

But it is not only neceffary to abolifh, or nearly to abolifh *, this artificial wealth, which, by heightening all prices, tends actually to impoverifh the ftate, and confequently to weaken government, it is alfo neceffary, without delay, to augment the fubftantial wealth of the nation, and thereby to bring the prices of neceffaries to correfpond to the exifting rate of wages. At prefent, and for many years back, the attention to augment the nominal wealth of the nation, feems to have greatly exceeded the attention to augment the fubftantial and phyfical wealth of the nation. A little, at a high price, has moft impolitically been preferred to much at a low price. Now the very object of true policy is, to have the fubftantial and phyfical wealth permanently abundant, becaufe, in proportion as that wealth is abundant or fcanty, fo will be the natural ftrength or weaknefs of a ftate.

The abundance of phyfical wealth, and the rate

* I fay nearly to abolifh; for there is, I think, a poffibility of inftituting country banks fo as not to be prejudicial to the nation.

or market value of that wealth, ought ever to be confidered diftinctly. If the land proprietor, from whom this wealth originates, and the ftatefman will confider thefe two things feparately, they will both readily acknowledge that the former ought to be the firft object of purfuit, as much as abundance of water ought to be a firft object of purfuit to the proprietor of a water-mill. This phyfical wealth, whatever be its rate, is the power that regulates the whole of the induftry of fociety. It cannot effect more by being rated high, nor will it effect lefs by being rated low; but if its quantity be increafed, the power thence arifing will be proportionally increafed.

A garrifon, fupplied with 20,000 facks of flour, may be expected to hold out a fiege twice as long as if it were fupplied with only 10,000 facks of flour; but it would be juftly deemed a moft abfurd and extravagant idea to think of ftrengthening the garrifon, not by fupplying it with 20,000 facks of flour, but by doubling the price of the 10,000 facks. If it be wife and prudent to ftrengthen a garrifon, not by increafing the price of the fupply which it poffeffes, but by increafing the quantity of that fupply, it will be no lefs wife and prudent to ftrengthen a nation in the fame manner; that is, not by increafing the price of the fubftantial wealth, which it produces, but by increafing the quantity of that wealth*.

There

---

* Prefuming that it will not be unacceptable to my learned readers, I fhall here remark, that Longinus, not being an

Econo-

There is not, at present, a complaint more general among all classes of men than that there is hardly any living, because all things are become so extravagantly dear. There is, however, a possibility that all things might become extremely plentiful, and consequently extremely cheap, and the system of the Economists leads to that. A common complaint, even among the rich, is, that the keeping of a horse is at present extremely expensive, oats and fodder are become so immoderately dear. Now the fact is, that the keep of a horse is in reality not dearer at present than it was 500 years ago; nay, perhaps is even cheaper; for 500 years ago it might have required the produce of three acres, but, from the improvements in agriculture, the produce of two acres may perhaps now suffice. In like manner, the maintenance of a regiment of soldiers is probably not more in reality

---

Economist, has, in sect. 29 of his Essay on the Sublime, misunderstood Plato, and censured him improperly. After having praised the rhetorical figure of circumlocution, and observed that in the use of it Plato was δαιος, or very eminent, he says he was accused by some of using it sometimes very improperly, as in the following expression, In a state, no gold wealth or silver wealth ought to be admitted. The mockers, who thought the word wealth might have sufficed, alleged, that he might just as well, in prohibiting cattle to be purchased, have said, *No sheep wealth,* and *no oxen wealth.* Plato's circumlocution, however, is here most apposite and emphatic. He placed the riches of a state in something else than gold and silver; and though he banished them from his common-wealth, he by no means excluded the physical wealth flowing from agriculture; and therefore he particularly distinguishes the kind of wealth which he would have to be excluded.

now

now than it was 150 years ago, but the parliamentary eftimates, and exceedings of eftimates, prove that the pecuniary expence of prefent days is far beyond what it was 150 years ago; that government accomplifhes not fo much with 20 millions as it formerly did with 5 millions, and that it is now actually experiencing the impotence of pecuniary wealth.

Other political writers, befides Mr. Young, have been deluded by the notion of the great importance of high price. The following falfe computation of Davenant has been repeated, with eulogiums, by fubfequent writers. 'In the year 1600,' fays Davenant, ' the whole rental of England did not exceed ' 6 millions, and the price of land was 12 years pur-' chafe; in 1688 the rental was 14 millions, and the ' price of land 18 years purchafe, fo that within ' this period, the land rofe from 72, to 252 ' millions.' A modern author, by the fame way of computing, reckoned the value of the lands of England a few years ago at 700 millions, that is, according to him, the lands of England are near ten times as valuable now as they were in the end of Queen Elizabeth's reign. This the Economift affirms to be a moft grofs mifcalculation, fimilar to that of doubling the price of the fupply of a garrifon, inftead of doubling the fupply; for, in the time of Elizabeth, England fed and clothed 4 millions of people; and at the prefent day can hardly feed and clothe 8 millions of people; confequently the real rife of value of its lands is barely double. But, if inftead of multiplying money, and thereby needlefsly raifing prices, we had been ftudious for thefe 200 years paft to have

multiplied

multiplied fubftantial and phyfical wealth by an unremitting encouragement of agriculture, the lands of England at this moment might perhaps have been near four times as valuable as in the time of Elizabeth, that is, they might now be feeding and clothing 15 or 16 millions of inhabitants.

Mr. Young's ill-grounded fondnefs for high price leads him to undervalue or decry low price or cheapnefs, without, however, explaining by any kind of illuftration, the prejudice that low price would bring upon a community. He makes affertion fupply the place of argument, and fays, p. 82, ' Cheapnefs of ' provifions is fuch an encourager of idlenefs, that ' no manufactures can ftand under it.' Now, fo far from this affertion being confiftent with fact, cheapnefs of provifions is the very thing that enterprifing mafter manufacturers above all things wifh for. It is the load-ftone that draws manufactures to itfelf. It has drawn the woollen manufactures even away from the woollen counties into the North; it has removed the gauze manufacture from London to Paifley; and the blanket manufacture from London to Dundee. What cheapnefs of provifions is in fome places, cheapnefs of coals is to Briftol, Newcaftle, Birmingham, and Carron. Were coals to be as dear in thofe places, as in fome parts of the kingdom, can it be doubted but their glafs works and iron works would quickly decline. Were a manufacturer of Birmingham to be afked whether he would wifh coals and provifions to be dear there, he would probably anfwer by the following queftion: Sir, would you wifh to ruin our town?

The same that cheapness or low price effects within the island, it effects throughout the whole commercial world. What turned the channel of the sugar trade from the British to the French Colonists, but because these last sold for 50 livres, what the British Colonists asked 50 shillings for. What else but cheapness brings rice and sugar to Britain from the East Indies, by a voyage of near 10,000 miles? What has brought American wheat, produced 300 miles from the sea, to Europe, but its cheapness? What but cheapness brings Russian iron to Britain, loaded with an inland carriage of 1000 miles? With these, and twenty other examples of the same kind before our eyes, shall we expect to invite foreign customers by high prices? We wish greatly to extend our foreign commerce, and at the same time we have many commercial rivals. Now internal high price has actually the effect of a bounty bestowed by us on those foreign rivals against ourselves. By our high prices we thus in effect say to the Swedes, We shall promote the sale of your herrings in foreign markets, in preference to our own, by keeping our own herrings 3 shillings a barrel dearer than yours.

In all things, a medium is best; therefore I doubt not but the following observation, made 100 years ago by the judicious Mr. Cary, of Bristol, will meet with approbation. ' The price of wheat,' he says, ' arises from the price of land; and the price of ' labour from the price of provisions; you cannot ' fall wages unless you fall product; but no good ' in running it down too low.' Supposing that at present we have raised a barrier against many foreign customers,

customers, by our high prices, which they find 5 or 6 per cent higher than those of our commercial rivals, it would be no detriment to the nation to remove that obstacle, not only by lowering our prices that 5 or 6 per cent, which would bring them to a par with those of our commercial rivals, but to lower them likewise 5 or 6 per cent even below that par. This would still be consistent with Mr. Cary's rule, and would give to foreigners a most decided preference to the British market. Mr. Young sees nothing but national perdition in lowering of prices; but from his own reasoning on the subject of the price of wheat it may be concluded, that previous to the late scarcity, that price was in effect one third lower than in the end of the last century. And since the invention of spinning mills, the price of cotton goods is fallen 50 per cent. As neither of these circumstances has brought any inconvenience upon the public, it may be presumed that the extension of the same system to other articles would not be accompanied with any detriment to the community. The encouragement of agriculture, and the inducement to reproduction, is not high price, but great consumption, which arises from general industry; for with high price, there may be little consumption and great want.

Those who measure the value of things by high price, are but too much inclined to run in search of that high price, in preference to the promoting of physical abundance, which is the very prop of society. Because in Covent-Garden-market green figs are about 40 times dearer than they are at Naples,

ples, would it be juft from thence to conclude, that London is 40 times richer in that article than Naples. Thofe who make high price the ftandard of national opulence, naturally drop into fuch an erroneous conclufion, and, by their way of reckoning, an acre of garden-ground in the north parts of Scotland is twice as valuable as in the neighbourhood of London; for by the ftatiftical ftate of Scotland, it appears, that in the north fome garden-ground is rented at the rate of 8l. per acre. This rent, however, is more likely to be the ftandard of the oppreffion of that part of the country, than of its profperity; for it may well be prefumed that an acre of garden-ground in the vicinity of London, rented at no more than 4l. would yield a greater quantity of produce than could be procured from an acre of garden-ground in the north. A great part of the enormity of this oppreffive rent would be done away, if, according to the natural fyftem of taxation for government fupply, one fifth, or one fixth of it, were appropriated to the defence of the ftate, as thofe that are now heavily taxed by that high rent, would then be relieved from other taxes.

I fhall conclude this point, at prefent, with the following remark. Mr. Young fays, p. 245, That high price enables landlords to raife their rents, and thereby to reimburfe themfelves for their taxes. But it may be afked of Mr. Young, why fhould landlords be reimburfed their taxes, any more than their tenants are reimburfed the 33 per cent, or the 25 per cent, which they pay to them for leave to cultivate the ground. The indemnification of every man

for

for the taxes paid by him, is internal peace and external defence. Can any man reasonably expect to enjoy those two great blessings for nothing?

Another of Mr. Young's erroneous doctrines, or rather ignorant positions, which I shall now proceed to examine, is the following; that taxes on consumption ought to have the preference to other taxes, for this most superficial reason (alleged also, as we have seen before, by Montesquieu), ' That ' they are paid by the consumers.' There he and Montesquieu rest, having satisfied themselves, that they have explained the nature of taxes on consumption. The consumers pay them. Neither he nor Montesquieu condescend to inform their readers what it is that enables the consumer to be a consumer, though upon that very point rests the distinct explanation of the whole of the expenditure of the kingdom. What should we think of a guide to the castle of truth, who should say to the enquiring traveller, this road leads directly to it through that dark and pathless wood. When you enter the wood, you must find your way to the castle in the best manner you can. Exactly such guides are Montesquieu and Mr. Young. They cease giving information precisely where it is most wanted. Who doubts, that taxes upon consumption are in the first instance paid by the consumer; but does that lead to any final political result in regard to the real fund for such taxes? Not in the smallest degree. When a school-boy purchases a folding knife, or a cricket bat, he is certainly the consumer in the first instance. The Economist, however, not only asks who furnished him with mo-

ney

ney to be a consumer; but who furnished the money to the person who supplied the school-boy, and who furnished the money to that third person, and who to the fourth, the fifth, the sixth person, &c. and by such a reiterated investigation, he will in the end trace the money to the sale of some of the agricultural produce of the earth. And he defies Mr. Young, or any other person, to draw the money disbursed by the school-boy from any other fund, besides that fund (the mines of the precious metals alone excepted), a fund which was not in existence last year, that will perhaps be wholly consumed this year, but will be reproduced next year, by the fertility of the soil, in conjunction with the labours of the cultivator. In like manner, it will be found, that the money disbursed by the blacksmith, the mason, the carpenter, and every other artisan, as consumers, may be traced to the same fund; and if in consequence of taxes on consumption, that money is twice as much as it otherwise would have been, that twice as much will occasion the original fund to be rated double in commercial value; but will not increase the fund.

Were a modern financier to say to a carpenter, your wages of two shillings a day allows you to be a consumer; I mean, therefore, by laying taxes on consumption, to draw four-pence or six-pence a day from you, the carpenter might very justly reply, You will in that be much deceived; for when I find articles of consumption taxed, I and all my fellow workmen will insist upon half-a-crown a day as wages; and that new demand will be most reasonable, for when we
had

had two fhillings a day, we had not, at the end of the year, one fhilling of furplus, neither fhall we have more, out of our half crown. The whole body of artifans throughout the kingdom is reprefented by that carpenter, as are all others who give their labour for wages; for thofe wages in a populous country actually meafure themfelves by the daily or annual fubfiftence of the receivers, without any regard to the pecuniary value of that fubfiftence.

Were Mr. Young upon his idea, that there is no need of enquiring what enables the confumers to become confumers, to propofe to the French loyalifts, now refugees in England, to become greater confumers, in order that government might be more benefited by them, they might, perhaps, reply in the following manner. Alas, Sir, it is not in our power to be greater confumers; the bloodthirfty tyrants at Paris have treated us as Hercules treated the giant Antæus; they have removed us from our Parent Earth; and inftead of being confumers, we are ready to perifh. Let us but touch again our Mother Earth, and we fhall revive, and become confumers. There is no other means but that.

In order to avoid needlefsly enlarging my prefent difcourfe, I fhall omit taking notice of feveral of Mr. Young's fmaller errors, the mere offspring of his falfe principles in effential points, and I fhall conclude my remarks upon his Political Arithmetic with expofing the futility of what he deems the unfurmountable objection to the *fingle tribute* or fingle tax propofed by the Economifts.

nomifts. Like Mr. Neckar, he falls into the blind miftake of making the general amount of the prefent taxes the ftandard or meafure of the fum total to be required by government, if all the taxes were to be confolidated into a fingle land tax. Becaufe the taxes at prefent raifed by Government, added to the annual loans, required during a war, exceed the amount of the land rents of Great Britain, he concludes, the fingle tribute propofed by the Economifts would abforb the whole of thofe rents, and not leave one farthing of income to the land proprietors, nay, would even occafion an annual deficit to government. Mr. Necker is more moderate in his computation; and upon a comparifon of the income of the land rents of France with the amount of its taxes, concludes, that the fingle tribute would run away with only 17 fhillings in the pound of the rents. But neither of thefe authors advert to circumftances which totally overturn their conclufions. The fingle tribute of the Economifts arifing from the furplus produce of the foil has nothing at all to do with the amount of modern taxes, become cumberfome by artificial price, accumulated upon artificial price, in confequence of a Public Debt of near 400 millions, which, according to the fyftem of the Economifts, would not at this moment have had any exiftence. The queftion with Mr. Neckar and Mr. Young ought to have been, Will four fhillings in the pound of the rents of land fuffice for the defence of the ftate in all prefumable emergencies; and for Great Britain, at leaft, the following computation, I think, will fhew, that the anfwer may be be in the affirmative, and will prove not only the great moderation, but the great efficacy of this tax. The rent of the land owners I shall state at only 1-4th of the general produce; and four shillings in the pound of that rent demanded by Government, is one 1-5th of it. Now 1-5th of 1-4th is equal to one 1-20th; that is, a land tax of four shillings in the pound would be equivalent to one shilling in the pound of the whole national income. In Great Britain are reckoned 72 millions of acres, and upwards. Now, of those 72 millions of acres, suppose 16 millions to be of little or no value, and that 16 millions more are required for horses, this will leave 40 millions for the sustenance of man. Of those 40 millions of productive acres, one twentieth, or two millions of acres are demanded by government for defence. This government share, therefore, allowing eight acres for the sustenance of one man, would enable Great Britain to maintain 250,000 men. But it may be said that a war establishment would require more than 250,000 men. I allow it. But would not a peace establishment require much fewer; therefore joining the two together, and taking the average, that average would be found not to exceed a land tax of four shillings in the pound; nay, would probably not exceed three shillings in the pound.

The following computation, I think, will prove, that if since the revolution a true assessment of the land tax had taken place, and a real four shillings in the pound had been raised on the rents of land in Great Britain, we should, previous to the commencement of the present war, have been entirely free from

any

any national debt. From Sir John Sinclair's valuable History of the Publick Revenue, part 2d. page 63, it appears that the national debt, on the 31st of December, 1701, was 16,394,702 pounds, that is about eleven years after the syftem of borrowing began. But fuppofing the land tax, from its firft eftablifhment, to have been not a nominal but a real four fhillings in the pound, and confequently to have amounted to one million a year more than it actually produced, this new national debt would thereby have been diminifhed eleven millions, and would have been, in December, 1701, only 5,394,702l. The war of the fucceffion, in Queen Anne's time, occafioned a further augmentation of the publick debt, which is ftated in the above mentioned hiftory at 54,145,363l. on the 31ft of December, 1714, but from this muft be deducted, firft, the preceding eleven millions, and fecondly, thirteen millions more, which the land tax, at a real four fhillings, would have produced from 1701 to 1714. Thefe deductions, then, would have left the publick debt, at Queen Anne's death, at no more than 30,145,363l. Soon after the death of King George I. that is, in 1727, the national debt, by the fame hiftorian, is ftated at 52,092,235l. but from the preceding obfervations, from this fum of 52,092,235l. the 24 millions before paid off are to be deducted, and likewife a million per annum, for 14 years, furnifhed by the land tax at a real four fhillings in the pound, confequently in December, 1727, the amount of the national debt would have been only 14,092,235l. Twelve years afterwards, when the Spanifh war broke

out

out in 1739, the national debt is ftated at 46,954,623l. but the reductions in the preceding periods would have taken from this debt 38 millions, and reduced it to 8,954,623l. while in the fame period, the annual million arifing from the land tax at a real four fhillings would have given a fupply of 12 millions, which would have extinguifhed the whole debt, and left above the fum of 3 millions as a furplus in the Exchequer. By the fame computation, the national debt in December, 1790, which is ftated at 247,833,236l. would have been really only 170,719,685l. This, it may be faid, is far fhort of a complete extinction of the national debt in 1790. But the following confiderations will ferve to prove, that on this point the means would have been adequate to the end. Mr. Brifcoe, who exactly 100 years ago publifhed feveral judicious remarks upon the new funds, proves by arithmetical tables, that for the loans of 1,000,000l. in 1692, and 1,200,000l. in 1693, Government actually bound itfelf to pay back 32 millions. Now, if the land tax had produced one million more each of thofe years, thofe two loans would not have taken place, and 32 millions of the national debt would have been thus prevented. Again, I have taken the land tax at a real four fhillings, as producing only one million more than it now produces; but for thefe laft fifty years it might juftly have been taken as producing annually two additional millions; confequently, thefe additional fifty millions, joined to the annual favings upon the intereft operating at compound intereft, which I have not reckoned upon, would have done

much

much more than liquidate the above 170,719,685l. of national debt.

Should the heavy expences of a war oblige government in future to have recourse to a loan, that loan, like those in King William's time, would be inconsiderable, and whatever debt was contracted during the war, it is plain from the preceding reasoning ought in time of peace to be liquidated by the land tax, by keeping that tax at such a rate above the peace establishment, as might afford a considerable annual reimbursement, till the whole new debt were paid off. This the land owners would find the cheapest expedient for themselves; for by avoiding the repetition of taxes on consumption, they would avoid the artificial price, thereby added to commodities, a heavier burden upon them than a direct land tax.

Having thus established, by reasoning which appears to me conclusive, the fundamental principle, That the primary and essential source of the Wealth of a Nation is the produce of its soil procured by the labour of the husbandman; and having also illustrated the consequence arising from that principle, That the supply for the defence of the state ought naturally to be drawn from the surplus of that produce, as being the only dispofeable revenue in the community, I shall now, for the further satisfaction of my readers, proceed to confirm what I have said relative to the national supply by an appeal to facts.

The system of the Economists, as appears from the preceding pages, tends to sweep away the whole of the taxes enumerated in Kearsley's Tax Tables, to abolish

abolish all Excises, all Stamps, in short, to extinguish all taxes but the Land Tax and the Customs, nay, even if possible not to spare the Customs. To this, some who make modern usages the measure of possibilities, will be apt to object as a new and unheard of theory, which no practice could ever realize. No; the Economist replies, so far from being a new theory, it is only a revival of the system of ancient days, with all the improvements that modern times render that system susceptible of. The French writers who have treated of this subject, have not done justice to it, in considering it as the new discovery of modern times. It is no more a new discovery than the discovery of Copernicus, in regard to the planetary system, which was known to the Pythagoreans two thousand years before. The doctrine of the Economists may now have been explained more fully than heretofore; yet imperfectly as it might have been formerly understood, it was, nevertheless, the rule of practice not only of this nation, but of many other civilized nations of Europe and Asia.

The system of the Economists, I have said, leads to sweep away the whole of the taxes enumerated in Kearsley's Tax Tables, and to abolish the Excises and Stamps. Now, I would ask my readers, if any of those taxes were known to Queen Elizabeth. Did either the Excises or Stamps then exist; and yet that Queen during her long reign shewed no small vigour both in defence and offence. Let the military efforts, exerted by Queen Elizabeth, at the head of 4 millions of subjects, with Scotland and Ireland so far from aiding her, hanging as heavy burdens

dens upon her, and without any West Indian or East Indian resources, be compared with the military efforts of Great Britain and Ireland during the present war, enjoying both West Indian and East Indian resources, and a population exceeding 13 millions of people, and it will be hard to decide, whether the former were any way inferior to the latter, in proportion to their respective funds, and the duration of the efforts. The foreign enemy of Queen Elizabeth was among the most formidable powers in Europe; but so far were the people of England then from being panic struck with the Grand Armada, they encountered it with an undaunted spirit at sea, and prepared with an equal spirit to encounter it at land. The English nobility and gentry came forward both with their purses and persons, on the principle, that their own safety and the safety of the state were inseparable*. So far was her revenue from

---

* I cannot here omit taking notice of the noblenefs of spirit of Lord Romney, who in the House of Lords, on the 27th of last March, proposed, instead of a Public Loan, to support government by a general subscription, to which he offered to contribute 5000l. In Ireland, likewise, we lately have instances of an equal public spirit. On the debate on a loan for this year in the House of Commons of that kingdom, Mr. Bagwell said, that rather than agree to a loan, he would give for the support of government the fourth of what he was worth, as long as the state should need it. Mr. Brown, another member likewise opposing the loan, said, that he would not lend, but give to government a sum without debenture, without treasury bill, or any other security. These gentlemen, whether from the knowledge of the true principle of supply, or from a momentary and very laudable zeal, have precisely hit the right nail on the head. There needs nothing more to prevent all future public loans, but that

from being exhausted by her perpetual struggles for forty years, that her treasury frequently overflowed, and she even declined accepting subsidies that were offered to her by Parliament. Upon enquiring into the chief sources of that revenue, we find that they consisted in the monied value of the produce of the soil, paid either by the direct tenants of the Crown, or by the land owners, in Parliamentary subsidies or feudal services. No Excises, no Stamps, nor any of the taxes enumerated by Kearsley, made part of that revenue. The possibility of defending the kingdom in great emergencies, by means of a land tax, without any of those taxes, and without burdensome loans, must therefore be admitted.

The Saxons, it appears from the History of England, by their trinoda necessitas, or three-fold obligation, laid the charge of defending the state on the possessors of land. It was a fundamental law among them, that all the lands of the kingdom, even those that were held by ecclesiastics and women were subject to three public duties, the building and repairing of forts and castles, the building and repairing of bridges, and the military expedition, which three duties, or trinoda necessitas *nulli unquam relaxari potest*, can be forgiven to no man.

From the constitution established by William the Conqueror, which in its fundamentals remained unaltered till the 12th year of Charles the Second's reign, that every proprietor of land in Great Britain and Ireland should adopt the spirit of Lord Romney, of Mr. Bagwell, and of Mr. Brown, and act accordingly. When the land proprietors shall connect themselves more with government, and government shall disconnect itself more from the money lenders, the athletic vigour of the nation will increase, and all apprehension of a financial convulsion will vanish.

the

the defence of the kingdom was placed wholly upon the revenue of land, exclufive of the trifling fupply which the Cuftoms yielded. But was England then in a ftate of weaknefs, becaufe it had no Excifes, no Stamps, nor any of that variety of taxes mentioned in Kearfley's Tables. Far otherwife. The conftitutional defence of England was then very great, and its King one of the richeft and moft powerful Monarchs in Europe. A contemporary author mentions, that the daily receipt of his Exchequer exceeded 1000l. fterling of that age, or above 3000l. of the prefent money*. Another author, anceftor of the prefent Earl Fortefcue, and contemporary with Edward the Fourth, fpeaking of the revenues of that King after he had made a refumption of the Crown lands that had been fraudulently alienated, fays, 'The King our fovereyng Lord had by tymes fithing 'he reigned upon us live-loode in Lordfhippis lands, 'tenements, and rents, nere hand to the value of 'the fifth part of his realm, above the poffeffions of 'the chirche.' What, then, fhould hinder Great Britain from being rich and powerful, were it now to abolifh all the prefent chaos of taxes, and revert to the fame fource of fupply, which formerly fufficed for all its exigencies, and which probably in thofe times, from the unimproved ftate of the lands, was a fource not half fo abundant as it would now prove. By the conftitution of England eftablifhed at the conqueft, which remained its conftitution, till it was moft impolitically overturned in the 12th year of

* See the Hift. of the Pub. Rev. of the Brit. Empire, vol. I. p. 44, 45.

Charle

Charles the 2d. by the act for the abolition of tenures, every poffeffor of lands was bound to give a regulated part of his income for the defence of the ftate; and if he neglected to give that regulated part, he in confequence forfeited his lands. Baron Gilbert, in his treatife on the Exchequer, fays, in conformity to many authorities, ' Whoever held lands by Knights
' fervice, and failed coming to attend the King in
' arms, according to the array that was made on
' every expedition, or failed to render his quota of
' men according to his tenure, his lands were origi-
' nally liable to be feized into the King's hands for
' not doing his duty.' The poffeffion of land, and the duty were infeparably connected together; and notwithftanding the duty, which fometimes exceeded four fhillings and five fhillings in the pound, the grant of the land was called *Beneficium*, or a Kindnefs.

It is then moft evident that this fingle tribute or fingle land-tax did not appear an abfurd thing either to the Anglo-faxon monarchs, or to thofe who immediately fucceeded them, fince they placed the whole of the defence of the kingdom upon it. The feudal fyftem, which confirmed that mode of taxation, was in its very nature a fyftem of union, calling upon all land poffeffors, wherever fituated within the dominions of the Sovereign, to affift him in defending the ftate in proportion to the landed property they poffeffed. Thus Henry the 2d, when he obtianed poffeffion of Ireland, firmly and irrevocably united that ifland to England by the fiefs and benefices which he there eftablifhed, *holding of the Crown*

of

of England*. That is to say, he conferred the same rights and the same privileges upon his new subjects in Ireland as those of England possessed, and precisely the same burdens, likewise, upon the land owners of both countries. The taxes placed by the feudal system upon the produce of land were precisely the same in both islands, and the tenants in capite, whose lands lay in Ireland, were bound by their tenures to give their fixed supplies to the Crown of England. In point of taxation, there was not one law for the land possessors in England, and another for those of Ireland, but both paid proportionably upon the same scale †. This

---

* The grants of lands in Ireland by the successors of Henry II. were held by the same tenure. The Butlers received the county of Ormond from Edward III. *as a fief of the Crown of England.* Fitz Eustace received the Barony of Castle-martin, in the county of Kildare, from Edward IV. *as a fief of the Crown of England.* Donald M'Arty More, in 1565, accepted of his lands from Queen Elizabeth, to hold them *as a fief of England.* Queen Elizabeth also gave to Sur le Boy, four estates in the county of Antrim, with the castle of Dunluce, as a fief of the Kings of England, &c. &c. See Sir John Davis.

† The subject of the American dispute always appeared to me to be most completely misunderstood by both parties in Great Britain, as well as by the revolters in America, from the true principle of government supply being misunderstood or gone into oblivion. Had that principle been known and attended to by those who drew up the Colony Charters, a permanent connection might have been formed between the mother country and the colonies, profitable yet unvexatious to both. About the commencement of the dispute, it was recommended to Lord North, as a means of restoring quiet and contentment, and as a permanent bond of union between the mother country and the colonies, to grant to the latter an entire liberty of foreign commerce, and an assurance of perpetual exemption of all taxation from the mother country, on condition that they should triple

their

This folves the hitherto unfolvable riddle of the Irifh peers fitting in the parliaments of England. As thofe peers held their fiefs of the crown of England, they took their feats in the parliament of England as poffeffors of thofe fiefs; and to have talked of a peer of one country being a commoner in the other, would then have been deemed the moft abfurd of all political folecifms. The king of the Irifh ever fince the time of Henry II. is he who wears the crown of England; and fo fenfible were the Irifh of this fundamental truth, that they even eftablifhed it when they were efpoufing the caufe of an impoftor; for Lambert Simnel, when he met with little countenance elfewhere, went to Dublin, where he was, with much folemnity, crowned king, not of Ireland, but of England. The Irifh were then fenfible of their relation to England, which ftill remains unaltered, and is ftedfaftly fupported by thofe who underftand the conftitution of both countries.

But it was not in England and Ireland alone that the fyftem of the Economifts, in regard to taxation, was anciently eftablifhed. In Scotland, when the Queen Regent, in 1555, propofed to raife a tax

---

their quit rents for the general defence of the empire. Henry the Second, if America had been fettled in his time, would probably have colonized it, as he connected Ireland with England. But the legal ignorance of the conftitutional nature of tenures that prevailed throughout the laft century, added to the felfifh fpirit of mercantile monopoly, led government into the abfurdity of eftablifhing the colonies by foccage tenures, and limiting their foreign trade.

upon

upon property in general, the gentry with much spirit obliged her to drop the defign, faying, that as for ages paſt the defence of the country had lain upon them, there was no occaſion for any alteration. Did not the fame fyſtem in former times prevail in France, in Germany, in Italy, and indeed over all Europe. Does not China at this moment adopt it! Has it not exiſted for ages in the empire of the Mogul. Do not at this day two-thirds of the revenue of Bengal ariſe from a tax upon the produce of the foil? Was any other tax known in that province, when it came under the power of Great Britain? And did not the firſt introduction of the tax upon falt occaſion much murmuring and much diſtreſs among the inhabitants, when according to the principles of the Economiſts, and the eſtabliſhed mode of that country, the whole of the fupplies ought to have been drawn from the zemindars, the receivers of rents, though not the proprietors of lands, the fovereign being the only proprietor. Even among ourfelves, about the period of the Revolution, a direct land-tax formed one-half of the taxes of England, though now making ſo ſmall a proportion of the general amount of thofe taxes. And in Scotland, at the time of the Union, about one-third of its public revenue confifted in a land-tax.

The preceding hiſtorical obfervations I think moſt clearly evince that the fyſtem of the Economiſts, in regard to taxation, is no new impracticable theory. It is at this moment practifed in countries of great extent, and in England, both before and after the Conqueſt, it was the fyſtem by which the
national

national supplies were regulated. The principle of that system has formerly in England been supported with great strictness; for it has been the repeated decision of lawyers, that should the king grant a tenure in the express words, *absque aliquid inde reddendo;* yet the law would imply a military duty; and in the Abbot of St. Bartholomew's case, in the 14th of Henry VI. upon a grant made in the words, *tenendum si frankement come le Roy est en son corone,* it was decreed, that the patentee was not exempt from military service.

This service was commonly termed, *servitium consuetum et debitum,* the accustomed and bounden service, or duty incumbent upon those who were the possessors of land. How this *bounden duty* came not to *bind,* during the four or five succeeding centuries, is a subject worthy of being amply discussed by some philosophical historian, as it has never yet been treated of with such attention as it deserves*. How came William the Conqueror, who

* Sir John Dalrymple, not many years ago, published an Essay on Feudal Property, in which his claim of having treated the subject like a scholar and a gentleman will be most readily admitted. But ought he not likewise to have treated it as a politician? His researches seem confined to the investigation of the ever changing rights of the feudal tenants, who, aided by the subtlety of lawyers, were continually endeavouring to evade their obligations to the crown, and, at the same time, to rivet their oppressive claims upon their inferior vassals, many of which claims they retain to this very hour. In the consideration of feudal property, the first point to have been investigated was, what property belonged inalienably to the crown, next, the nature of the property belonging to the subject.

who had about five millions a year, and Edward IV. who had near four millions a year, to be succeeded by a King James and a King Charles, who had not much above half a million a year, though there was no conſtitutional alteration in the financical ſyſtem from the firſt of theſe monarchs to the laſt, and the monied value of commodities was riſen three fold.

The firſt cauſe of this depredation of royal revenue appears to have been the ſupine negligence of ſome of our kings, who not conſidering that by the conſtitution they really were but life poſſeſſors, gave away with both hands what they had no right to give away. What by Domeſday Book was *terra regis*, or kings land to Edward the Confeſſor, became kings land to William the Conqueror, who is ſaid to have poſſeſſed in royal domain 1,200 manors, which ſucceſſively became the right of the kings who reigned after him. But of thoſe 1,200 manors, Charles I. probably did not poſſeſs 100, all the others having been alienated by the impolicy of his predeceſſors. A ſecond cauſe of the depredation of royal revenue was the ſchool-boy notion of

ject, and for what cauſe, or for what expected ſervices it was beſtowed. If Sir John had taken but half the pains to elucidate the *Duties* of the feudal tenants that he has taken in treating of their *Rights*, he would have rendered his ingenious eſſay much more valuable. What he uniformly deems progreſs was in reality a degradation of the conſtitution then ſubſiſting. The feudal ſyſtem was a Public Edifice whoſe pins and mortiſes were daily weakening, and from whoſe roof ſome tiles were every year moſt knaviſhly ſtolen, to cover caſtles of private deſpotiſm.

eſtimating

eftimating wealth not by its phyfical ufe, but by its prefent value in money, and upon that notion agreeing to a permanent commutation of revenue in kind for revenue in prefent money to remain unalterable; in confequence of which the king of Great Britain now receives for fome lands one penny, in lieu of what fells in the market at prefent for five fhillings. A third caufe was the unwatchfulnefs of thofe who ought to have guarded the king's revenue, and thereby fuffering the moft fraudulent entries to be made by the feudal tenants. A fourth caufe, and the laft I fhall mention, was the unremitting endeavours of the feudal tenants to fmuggle and conceal the number and value of their fees, fo that in lefs than 300 years after the Conqueft, the number of them was diminifhed above one-half; and in Charles the Firft's time they hardly amounted to one-fourth of what they had been in the time of William the Conqueror, and thefe often rated at lefs than one-tenth of their real income. Mr. Philips, in his very curious treatife, entitled, *Tenenda non Tollenda*, written in 1660, againft the abolition of the feudal tenures, and abounding with legal knowledge, gives the following inftance of two of thofe fmuggled eftates: ' An eftate,' he fays, ' in
' the reign of Charles I. above 1000l. per annum,
' hath been found (by the Efcheators) to be but of
' the yearly value of twenty marks. Another eftate,
' confifting of very few manors and as few copy-
' holders, but moft in farms and demefnes, upon
' an improved and almoft racked rent, worth 6000l.
' per annum, found at no greater yearly value than
' 183l.

' 183l. 11s. which is lefs than the 30th part.' Had the records of the Exchequer, for fucceffive reigns, been faithfully kept, and were they ftill preferved unimpaired, who knows but among the land fmugglers of the reign of Charles I. might be found John Hampden, and others of the violent oppofitionifts of thofe times, fo clamorous for a redrefs of grievances, the chief of which they themfelves occafioned by unconftitutionally withholding their *debita fervitia*, or bounden fervices from government. What fhould we think of the tenants of a Duke of Bedford, who fhould combine to pay him only one-tenth or one-thirtieth of what was ftipulated in their leafes, or fhould burn their leafes, and deny to pay him any thing. But fuch tenants to the crown of England, and to the crown of Scotland, were the majority of the land proprietors of Great Britain in the reign of Charles the Firft. They had not only ftripped the crown of almoft all the royal domains, but had fhaken off their obligations to defend the ftate, by which they had rendered themfelves from an *effential clafs*, one of the moft *uneffential claffes* of fociety.

Thefe unconftitutional and difhoneft practices of the land proprietors, leaving King Charles the Firft with hardly any revenue, that ill advifed monarch not having the political prudence and fortitude to withftand fuch fraudulent violations of the conftitution, had recourfe to illegal means of fupply, which were the fource of many calamities to the nation. But no one acquainted with the Englifh hiftory will affirm that the calamities that then overwhelmed

whelmed the nation had no other fource befides the king's illegal conduct. The conftitution was not more violated by Charles, than by the acts and proceedings of thofe who with much bitternefs were contending for *rights*, without faying one word about *duties*. Would not Charles the Firft, when he granted the Petition of Rights, have been fupported by the conftitution, if he had addreffed the parliament to the following purpofe : ' It gives me
' great pleafure to have eftablifhed the rights of my
' people, but I muft reprefent to you that the
' crown alfo has its rights, and I expect this par-
' liament to confirm thofe rights. The Doomfday
' Book fhews us that my predeceffor, William the
' Firft, had in royal domain twelve hundred man-
' ors; now as there is by law no prefcription againft
' the crown, it muft be allowed that all thofe man-
' ors belong to me. Befides, as many frauds have
' been committed by changing military tenures for
' other holdings, and by great undervaluations of
' eftates upon the deaths of tenants in capite, I
' defire the parliament may appoint a committee to
' enquire into the defrauders of the public revenue,
' and to form a bill, to which I will give my affent,
' for preventing fuch frauds in future, that the
' defence of the nation may be put upon its old
' conftitutional footing.' In fuch an addrefs the king certainly would not have talked unconftitutionally; but his defpotic and tyrannic temper, and his overweening notion of the uncontrolable fupremacy of the kingly office, and perhaps a defire of copying after the example of his brother-in-law in

France,

France, who had been taxing his subjects for twenty-two years, without the authority of the states of his kingdom, led Charles to pursue other measures. The king's faults however by no means rendered the land smugglers faultless.

The mutual dislikes proceeding to animosities, both parties had recourse to arms, without either of them being able clearly to define upon what grounds they were fighting. But had the principles of the Economists been then understood by king and people, those bloody contentions needed not to have taken place; for by those principles not only the nature and source of the public supply would have been manifest to the whole nation, but the best mode of collecting it likewise; and all the alteration necessary for obtaining a free constitution would have been to have made the grants annual, according to the discretion of parliament, and the actual circumstances of the time, and the executive power accountable for the expenditure.

The issue of the fatal contest was the murder of the king, by a sentence in direct violation of law; and a succession of his chief murderer a few years afterwards to the despotic rule of the nation. Under the iron rod of this despot the supplies for national defence were collected without rule or measure by military compulsion; and, by various extortions, more money was raised by him in one year than had been raised by the murdered sovereign in three years.

Upon the restoration of Charles II. when it was supposed the ancient laws were restored with him,
and

and likewife the ancient mode of fupply, it might have been expected that the parliament, from the experience of paft troubles, would have adopted fuch means as might prevent land fmuggling in future; and while it renewed the obligation of the land poffeffors to furnifh their debita fervitia, or bounden fervices, in fome better mode than by feudal tenures, would at the fame time have laid the executive power under fome obligation to apply thofe debita fervitia to the defence and honour of the nation. Parliament however adopted a meafure altogether different, and not more contrary to the fpirit of the conftitution than to the dictates of found policy. By the moft abfurd and unconftitutional act for the abolition of tenures, it wholly exempted the land poffeffors from all direct fupplies whatever; and in commutation for what ought by the former conftitution, as well as by the dictates of juft policy, to have been drawn directly from the produce of land, it annexed hereditarily to the crown an excife duty on beer and ale, amounting not to one-twentieth of what by the old conftitution was required from the owners of land. This was a no lefs violent than impolitic innovation*. By diffolv-

---

* Among the many unconftitutional and oppreffive expedients of fupply adopted by the long parliament, the excife had been introduced by them, in imitation of the practice of Holland, which in this point had attracted the curiofity of many in England in the time of James I. who is faid to have fent over a perfon thither to enquire into the manner and management of it. About that time it was by the Englifh ftiled *Heathen Greek*, and was moft generally reprobrated by them.

ing the *nexus adictiffimus,* or bond of moſt ſtrict obligation, it threw the land owners into the claſs of mere idlers, a claſs ever to be avoided by a well conſtituted ſociety; and it introduced a new mode of taxation, rather prejudicial, in many caſes, to the nation at large, and no leſs burdenſome to numbers of individuals, than the feudal ſervices had been to the feudal tenants. I may likewiſe add, as it has ſince proved, no leſs intricate and perplexing in the modes of raiſing it, than the incidents of the feudal tenures ever had been. As a ſupplement to this firſt exciſe duty, the parliament granted an aſſeſſment upon the lands in the different counties; but inſtead of impoſing it in a juſt proportion to the fund to be taxed, (which is the fundamental principle of all equitable taxation) it was rated negligently and inaccurately, in conſequence of which ſome muſt have been too much charged, while others were too much eaſed.

At the era of the Revolution the parliament nobly reverted to the ſyſtem of nature, in regard to public ſupplies, and eſtabliſhed a land-tax ſufficient not only for the peace eſtabliſhment, but as has been proved in pages 84 and 85, for the exigencies of an expenſive war likewiſe; had the tax been levied in exact proportion to the value of the rents upon which it was impoſed. The Economiſts affirm that the produce of the land is the only fund for national ſupplies. The parliament at the Revolution made a great ſtep towards this important truth, when by eſtabliſhing a land-tax at four ſhillings in the pound, they declared the produce of land to be the

the chief fund for taxation. Eſt quoddam prodire tenus*. Why they omitted the principle of impoſing that tax in a juſt proportion to the reſpective rents, it may be now impoſſible to determine; but that ſuch a principle ſhould at this moment be neglected in the eſtabliſhment of a land-tax, is a great reproach to theſe enlightened times, and a great injuſtice to the majority of the land proprietors of the kingdom. A deviation from this principle in other matters, with the pretence of adhering to it, would be deemed no leſs ridiculous than unjuſt. In this reſpect the modern acts for the land-tax may be conſidered as political bulls of no ſmall magnitude. They eſtabliſhed diſproportion almoſt in the ſame paragraphs, where they enact that juſt proportion ſhall be obſerved; as if a landed gentleman ſhould ſay to his tenants, I mean that you ſhould pay me your rents in a juſt proportion to the ſize of your farms, that is, I require a certain quantity of wheat from each of your wheat fields, whether the field be large or ſmall, and a certain quantity of apples from each of your orchards, whether the orchard be large or ſmall, or whether the crop be ſcanty or plentiful. It would be readily allowed that this gentleman was not very accurate in his notions of proportion. But nearly ſimilar is the ſpirit of the preſent acts for raiſing a land-tax in Great

* From what is here remarked, as well as from what is above written, it moſt evidently appears, that Mr. Pitt, and thoſe who voted with him, in the affair of the Legacy Bill, acted more in conformity to the Revolution principles of taxation than thoſe who oppoſed that bill.

Britain.

Britain. From some they require only four-pence, and from some four shillings, by the same rule of proportion; nay, from some not even four-pence; for I can declare, upon good information, that a gentleman possessing an estate of 5,000l. a year, in one of the northern counties of England, pays in land-tax, at four shillings in the pound, only 75l. The undervaluation from a real four shillings in the pound on this single estate, if it had been brought to account in the Exchequer, since the Revolution, with the compound interest thence arising, would have liquidated upwards of one million of the national debt. We may thence discover the radical cause why the nation is at present so much involved, for if the deficiency upon a single estate of 5,000l. a year, would have sufficed to have paid off one million of the national debt; it would not be a strained conclusion to affirm, without any farther computation, that the sum total of the undervaluations of the land-tax upon the estates of the whole kingdom, would have paid off the whole national debt.

As the number of landed gentleman that are aggrieved by the present very disproportionate assessment of the land-tax far exceeds the number of those that are thereby unjustly favoured, it is most reasonable that this unfair advantage of the minority should give way to that of the majority. This majority therefore have a right to press for an equal valuation of the land-tax without delay, that the minority, who are now exempt, may bear an equal share of the public burdens with themselves. The equal

equal valuation of the affeffment, and the rate of the affeffment, are two very different things, and ought ever to be kept diftinct. The latter depends upon the difcretion of parliament, but the former is founded on a ftronger authority than that of parliament, the immutable law of right and wrong, to which law parliament ought ever ftudioufly to conform.

Leaving the rate of the affeffment, as it ought to be, indeterminate, unlefs by an annual law of parliament, I fhall here confine myfelf to the means of obtaining its equal valuation. For this purpofe there is no need of a new Doomfday Book, or any intricate mode of inveftigation. As the knowledge of the value of the fund is the fine qua non for obtaining a proportionate rate, and as the leafes to tenants, whether annual or for a term of years, difcover that fund, let all leafes of whatever kind be regiftered in the refpective counties where the lands are fituated; and let the affeffments be made for fuch county according to thofe regifters. Whenever a leafe is renewed, let the value of fuch new leafe be faithfully fpecified and regiftered within one month after its date, and publifhed three times in the newfpaper of the county town, or in the London Gazette; and let the particular new affeffment be made thereupon, by which eafy and honeft expedient, the income to government would rife or fall in exact proportion as the income of the land proprietors rofe or fell; or rather as the income of the whole nation rofe or fell; for it is to be prefumed that the rents of lands will only rife or decline as this laft rifes or declines.

The regiftration above propofed would effect the fame thing in politics, that logarithms have effected in mathematics. The now intricate and perplexing financial queftions would thereby be rendered eafy of folution. The affeffment of the poor-rates fuppofes fuch a notoriety in every parifh in England; and the fame notoriety is implied by the laws enjoining the payment of tythes; for that law could never have been put in effect with exactitude, were not every clergyman to be fully acquainted with the whole of the produce of his own parifh. When England was divided into knights fees, and the owners of them were bound in return to defend the kingdom, the notoriety of thofe fees was implied in the very inftitution; and the corruption of that inftitution proceeded from the neglect of notoriety, or the difficulty of obtaining it. The art of printing was then unknown, nay even the art of writing was almoft unknown; there were no newfpapers, no turnpike roads, no regular poftage of letters, confequently, though notoriety was the principle of the inftitution, deeds of darknefs eafily efcaped detection, and defrauders annually increafed, even with the connivance of the efcheators, who were fometimes only two for all England. The modern improvements in civil life, that have been juft mentioned, would not only preclude in thefe times any fraudulent evafions of the land-tax, but would render the levying of it a matter of the greateft eafe and correctnefs. Every county would have its receiver general refiding in the county town, correfponding with the exchequer, and making his remittances

mittances thither; and the financial machine would be kept at lefs expence, would move with more accuracy, and would feldomer require repairs and amendments, when thus compofed only of a a few wheels, than as it is at prefent, clumfily formed of an hundred wheels.

Having given an outline of the mode for eftablifhing an equal valuation of the land-tax, I fhall proceed to confider a fuperficial objection often made againft fuch a proportionate valuation, which objection has ferved as a ftumbling block to many who fincerely wifh to fee fuch a proportionate valuation take place. Many landed eftates, it has been faid, have been purchafed in counties where the valuation of the land-tax is extremely low, upon the prefumption that no alteration of that tax would take place, and now to impofe a higher rate upon fuch eftates would be an injuftice to their poffeffors. But is it not an injuftice in thofe poffeffors, who enjoy an equal protection of government with their neighbours, not to contribute to the fupport of government in an equal proportion with their neighbours. The *falus populi*, or the obligation of defence, is in its nature paramount to every other obligation. We have feen above, that in the feudal times a grant of land made with the exprefs condition of no fervices, *tenendum fi frankement come le roi eft en fon corone*, was neverthelefs judged in law not to be exempt fram military fervice; and the Saxons faid of their *trinoda neceffitas*, or threefold obligation, *nulli unquam relaxari poteft*, it can be forgiven to no man. Among the Romans likewife,

in

in the flourishing times of their republic, a free man who fraudulently avoided being enrolled in the legions, when called upon by the conful, was made a flave, and his property was confifcated to the ftate. Many purchafes of landed eftates were doubtlefs made in England between the Reftoration and the Revolution; but when the affeffment of the land-tax, foon after the Revolution, was raifed from 600,000l. which it had been at the Reftoration, to two millions, we do not find that thofe new purchafers were exempted in the new valuation. It is the protection of Government that renders any man's eftate valuable to him; and if in confequence of this protection, an eftate bought at twenty-five years purchafe fhould (without any improvement) become faleable for thirty-five years purchafe, government is certainly entitled to a retribution for fuch a benefit. The rife in value here fpecified amounts to upwards of one-fourth; but fhould an eftate now paying only four-pence in the pound, be required to pay a full four fhillings in the pound, that would not be quite one-fifth of augmentation, confequently the benefit beftowed by government would exceed the retribution to government, which (exclufive of any rife in marketable value of an eftate) would be entitled to four fhillings in the pound from it, if the other eftates of the kingdom were rated at four fhillings. But when government by drawing the fupplies from the direct fource fhall become independant of the monied men, whofe fhackles it has worn thefe hundred years paft, the rate of intereft will fink to fuch a degree

as

as will raife the marketable value of land in a greater proportion than I have above mentioned. To the objectors among the new purchafers of eftates at undervaluations, adminiftration might then fay, we will reimburfe you the full money you paid for your eftates, and will refel them, burdened with four fhillings in the pound, confident that the exchequer will be a gainer by fuch commutations. If the exchequer, as I think may be demonftrated, would be a gainer by the commutations of fuch eftates, it would then be the intereft of the prefent poffeffors of thofe eftates to avoid fuch commutations. This is confidering the fubject in the light of the objectors, as a mere money tranfaction, in which light it appears that fhould government maintain the nation in profperity, the impofition of four fhillings in the pound, would really take nothing out of their pockets. But the neceffity of defence, or in other words, of fupplies for defence, places the fubject in another light, in which though the objectors have not chofen to confider it, the conftitution muft. A perfon who buys an eftate does not only lay out his money in the purchafe of land, but actually enlifts himfelf as a defender of the ftate. We have feen above that government has actually been carried on, and confequently may be carried on, without any of thofe taxes, that are called taxes on confumption. Now fhould the Britifh government revert to that natural fyftem, abolifh all taxes on confumption, and draw the public fupplies from the direct fource of fupply, the produce of land, a land proprietor in fuch circumftances, stances, sitting exempt from a land-tax, would assist government no more than one of his own grooms. Upon what principle then could such a land proprietor expect the protection of government.

I shall conclude, at present, with one reflection more on this point. Were all our taxes on consumption suppressed, and the whole of the public supplies, as in former times, to be raised from land, the land proprietors would, nevertheless, still remain the most opulent class in society, as possessors of the only assured surplus revenue in the community. Merchants and manufacturers, by many years assiduous attention, may become rich, but they may likewise, by many mischances, become bankrupts. Those who live upon stipends and salaries, are presumed to have only a daily subsistence, correspondent to their respective ranks. In the present state of things, by the rise of prices and the fixedness of salaries, many of them have not even that daily subsistence; and by the extinction of taxes on consumption, they might be enabled to live in ease, but not in affluence. The great body of manual labourers give their whole capital daily to the public, without any reserve of interest; consequently, when infirmity or old age overtakes them, instead of having made accumulations, they are often in a state of destitution; and be the prices of things, or the rate of wages what they may, this will ever be the case with the great majority of them. Mental labourers, though by their ideas, not only individuals, but

nations

nations are often rendered rich, generally receive themselves but a scanty retribution. Laudantur & Algent. The British history furnishes many examples of the great opulence of our nobility and gentry, when no public taxes existed in this island but what were paid by themselves; which taxes, in the estimation of the payers, were not even deemed taxes, but stiled by them servitium liberum, that is, the service of a freeman. If such was the case in former times, when the marketable value of estates was low, in consequence of the rate of interest being ten per cent and upwards, it is reasonable to expect, that upon a return to that system, the landed gentlemen would be more distinguished for their opulence, from the marketable value of their estates being high, in consequence of the low rate of interest. Land, selling at thirty-six years purchase, is a capital three times more valuable than when sold at twelve years purchase.

Having in the preceding part of this discourse shewn that manufactures made and sold at home, though they may enrich individuals, do not give any augmentation of national revenue, I shall here make a few observations in respect to the profit that accrues to the nation from that idol of modern times, foreign commerce. If our imports are of equal value to our exports, the national gain will be nothing; it will only be as if a crown-piece were exchanged for five shillings, or five shillings for a crown. In this state of an equal balance between us and our foreign customers, though the nation

may

may be no gainer, yet our own merchants, and those of foreign countries who fell our merchandize may be great gainers, by putting 30, or 40, or 50 per cent upon the retail of the merchandize imported by them, and fold to their fellow-fubjects. Thus the Eaft-India company may gain annually 800,000 l. upon the fale of their teas, though the nation may thereby not gain a fingle farthing. This private gain, and others of the like kind, are too often maftakenly deemed national gains, though in fome certain cafes (as in the cafe of tea fome years ago) the nation is actually a lofer by them. The real national gain, therefore, cannot be eftimated from the moft accurate ftatements of the infpector general of the cuftoms, nor from the magnitude of the exports, if the magnitude of the imports keeps pace with it. To fettle this balance clearly, very many circumftances are neceffary to be taken into the account; and till thofe circumftances be minutely underftood, the decifions in regard to the profit from foreign commercial dealings muft be very inaccurate. Should this profit, in refpect of Great Britain, amount annually to five or fix millions, though it may be doubted whether it rifes fo high, that profit, in comparifon of the other part of the national revenue arifing from agriculture, would not be fo confiderable as to juftify the great importance annexed to it in the minds of the multitude, and far lefs to juftify government in engaging in war in compliance with the avaricious fpirit of thofe who wifh to extend their gains by unlawful

and

and unjuft means*. From the continual cry in the mouths of fome, *We are a commercial nation*, one would be inclined to think, that they believed the chief fource of the riches and profperity of Great Britain was her foreign trade; that without foreign trade poverty and diftrefs would overfpread the land, nothing but mifery would be known, and Great Britain would lofe her preponderance among the nations of the earth; therefore, every intereft fhould give way to the intereft of foreign trade. Whoever rightly underftands the principles of the Economifts, will fee no neceffity for fuch gloomy forebodings, even on the fuppofition of no foreign trade. The Economifts, however, are far from faying, Perifh our commerce; or from wifhing to adopt the fyftem of the antient Egyptians, who prohibited foreign trade; or applying to Great Bri-

---

* What we tranflate *Good-will towards men* (Luke 11 and 14) may, perhaps, be as juftly rendered *Good-will among men*. This Chriftian good-will among men has but too often been interrupted by a felfifh fpirit among dealers, of monopolizing foreign markets to themfelves, at the hazard of prejudice to the national welfare. The frequent captures of Englifh fhips by the Spanifh guarda cofta's greatly irritated the Britifh nation, and occafioned the war with Spain in 1739. But it may be doubted whether both nations were not betrayed into hoftilities by the avarice and artifice of our South Sea Company. From a perfon that refided feven years at Carthagena and other places in Spanifh America, before the breaking-out of that war, I have been told that the Spanifh guarda cofta's, that would otherwife have remained inactive, were privately excited by our S. S. Company to make feizure of Englifh fhips, who, as interlopers, fold goods to the Spanifh colonifts cheaper than the Company fold them.

tain

tain the late Biſhop Berkeley's maxim in regard to Ireland, and ſaying, Great Britain might be happy and proſperous, though it were to be ſurrounded by a wall of braſs 40 cubits high.

The Economiſts ſee not only national profit in foreign commerce rightly conducted, but a great augmentation of the conveniencies and enjoyments of human life. They, neverthelefs, confider foreign commerce as an object of very little regard as to revenue, in compariſon with that ariſing from the cultivation of territory; and deem a ſtate poſſeſſing an ample territory to be exceedingly miſled and ill-adviſed, that beſtows more of its attention upon commerce than upon agriculture, ſince this laſt is a much more ample and more ſubſtantial ſupport of national opulence and power than the former.

Many falſe principles of writers on commerce might here be quoted, but I ſhall mention only one. Great Britain, ſays one of thoſe writers ſeventy years ago, could no more expect to get rich without the balance of trade in her favour, than a family could get rich, the maſter of which had no other occupation than winning the money of his wife and children at play. In this writer's idea, then, which has ſerved as a miſleading doctrine to thouſands, Great Britain could not increaſe in opulence and proſperity without acquiring ſomething from her neighbours more than ſhe gives them. Were this doctrine true in regard to Great Britain, it would likewiſe be true in regard to other nations that have foreign traffic; and they ſhould all direct their views to acquire ſomething from their neighbours more than they give them. As it is impoffible they fhould all fucceed in this, the confequence of commercial dealings between different nations would then be, according to that falfe fyftem, that while fome of them were thereby enriched, others of them muft thereby be impoverifhed. By that fyftem, all the commercial nations of the earth are confidered as fo many gamefters, each endeavouring to make itfelf rich by making its neighbours poor; and what can be expected from this but continual jealoufies, diflikes, and animofities, rendering nations unfriendly, and but too frequently hoftile to each other. The Economifts, on the other hand, whofe leading principle is *Good-will among men*, affirm, that all the nations of the earth may traffic together with mutual advantage, without acquiring from each other more than they give to each other; and that Great Britain may daily advance in wealth and profperity, without gaining one farthing by her foreign trade, however extenfive that may be, provided fhe gives her attention to acquire every year additional wealth from her territory and her feas.

Do manufactures afford no revenue, and does foreign commerce yield but a fmall income—and do we poffefs what furnifhes the natural income of a ftate, an extenfive and fertile territory not much more than half cultivated, are we not then called upon by true policy to increafe the wealth and power of the ftate by rendering this territory more productive. It is to this new Potofi, this mine of riches, that the Economifts wifh to direct the attention of Britifh patriots, and Britifh agriculturifts.

Here

Here permanent wealth may be acquired without the sword, without the envy or molestation of our neighbours, accompanied with the increase of people, the lessening of taxes to individuals, but the augmentation of them to the state, and with the diminution of the number of poor, not by death, but by transferring them into the class of those living in easy and comfortable circumstances.

As the produce of the territory of a state is the natural support of its government, it becomes, therefore, the duty of government to establish such regulations as may contribute to render that territory as productive as possible. The dominium utile of the lands is secured to the possessors by government; but the dominium regale, inherent in government, is paramount to the other, and gives to government a right of inspection and direction over the whole. No land proprietor, in civil society, is entitled to say he may do with his estate what he pleases; because, should he, from obstinacy or negligence, omit to render his lands productive, the state is thereby so far endamaged, and consequently has a right to take such measures as may prevent that damage. This renders evident the great importance and necessity of the bill for the division and improvement of the commons and waste lands of Great Britain. By passing that bill (the fruits of the assiduous labours of the Board of Agriculture) into a law, the legislature will directly enlarge its own revenues, as well as those of individuals, and will thereby as much increase the power and
opulence

opulence of the nation, as if a fertile ifland half as large as Ireland were united to its territory.

But it is not only neglected lands, but the neglected cultivators of thofe lands, that call for the interpofition and protection of government. The legiflature, by taking upon itfelf the noble occupation of exempting from thraldom the poor and induftrious country labourers, would, in fact, be only looking more particularly after its own interefts, for the latter muft fuffer in proportion as the former are oppreffed. The nation is very much obliged to Sir John Sinclair, who, by his affiduous and pratriotic labours, has been inftrumental in bringing to the knowledge of the public the grievances and oppreffions fuffered by many of thofe cultivators in the northern parts of the ifland. There is hardly one of the many judicious and humane writers of the ftatiftical account of Scotland, whofe parifh is in the northern and mountainous parts, who does not enumerate among the difadvantages that agriculture there labours under, the high rents, and the want of fecurity to the farmers in the poffeffion of their farms.

In regard to high rents it may be obferved, that, according to the fyftem of the Economifts, government ought always to feel an immediate benefit from them, or from any rife of rent whatever. In that cafe, the malady and the remedy would go together, and the people at large would more wilingly pay double for their bread and their butchers-meat, when they perceived the income of government was thereby proportionably increafed, and

con-

consequently the less would be demanded from them through the means of other taxes. But when they find the prices of their bread and butchers-meat raised upon them without any alleviation in other taxes, the moderate naturally conclude that there is misgovernment somewhere, and the factious that government is to blame; when, in fact, it is government that is injured, as well as the community at large. A landed proprietor, who raises the rents of his farms without any actual improvement of them, what else does he do but assume the unconstitutional power of taxing his fellow-subjects without consent of Parliament, and his farmers are his tax-gatherers. When these ask ten-pence for a pound of butter which they formerly sold for five-pence, or demand six-pence for a pound of cheese which they before sold for a groat, and sell their corn and cattle proportionably dearer, what apology can they give for these new taxations but that they are compelled to impose them, because their landlord has asked so much more of them.

The rise of rents from a real improvement of the soil, and augmentation of its produce, is to be viewed in a quite different light. This rise of rents is a principal object of the Economists. It enlarges the powers of the main wheel, that moves every other wheel in society, and is itself set in motion by nature and the industry of man. As the motion of that wheel is progressive or retrograde, so, proportionally, is the prosperity of the state progressive or retrograde. A rise of rents after this manner ought as much to be encouraged by government,

vernment, as the other manner of raising rents ought to be condemned. How common is it to find those two very different meanings of the word improvement confounded together, not only by superficial reasoners, but by men who might be expected never to lose sight of the distinction between them. A man who has raised his estate, without any improvement of the soil, from 500 l. a year to 1000 l. makes no difficulty of saying he has improved his estate. But has he thereby improved the estate of the nation? By no means. He has only taxed the manufacturers and labourers in his neighbourhood, and rendered living more hard to them, till they overtake him by raising their prices and wages upon him, which restores all of them to the relative situation they were in before; when, should a new rise of rents in the former manner take place, the strife between them is recommenced without any benefit accruing from thence to the nation.

The increase of produce, and not the increase of the price of produce, is what a wise agricultural nation will chiefly aim at; and when this becomes the principal object of the land owners of Great Britain, the increase of their incomes will then be a certain proof of the flourishing state of the nation. The more they raise their rents after this manner, the more the people will have occasion to rejoice, as easiness of living and general abundance will be the consequence.

The nation, in general, being greatly interested that the rents of lands should be raised after this

manner

manner, the legiflature is therefore bound to purfue fuch meafures as may remove every obftruction that prevents its taking place. And as one of the chief obftructions to the increafe of national produce, upon which the public profperity fo much depends, is the want of leafes, that is, the want of fecurity to the cultivator in his farm, the legiflature, therefore, poffeffes the right of enforcing the granting of leafes throughout the whole kingdom.

It was well obferved by a member of the laft parliament, who has wide eftates in that part of the ifland where the grievance of the want of leafes is moft feverely felt, that agriculture ought to be under regulation as well as commerce. And certainly nothing can be a more difgraceful and abfurd policy in an agricultural nation, than that great numbers of owners of land fhould from negligence, miftaken avarice, or a luft of domination, be fuffered fo to let their land as to prevent the general yearly revenue of the ftate from augmenting twenty or thirty millions, more efpecially when by letting their lands upon leafes thofe very owners of land would probably foon greatly augment their prefent incomes. The mofaical law forbad the ox that treaded out the corn to be muzzled; but in fome parts of Great Britain the cultivators themfelves are muzzled; their labour, though yielding fuftenance to others, not yielding fuftenance to themfelves and families. This impolicy and inhumanity having long prevailed, has compelled many of them to become cultivators in America, from whence perhaps they have lately been inftrumental

mental in relieving our wants, thereby draining the money out of the kingdom, when by a different policy they might have been adding both to its wealth and its strength.

But the cultivators in that part of the island, it it alleged, are lazy and indolent. To this it may be answered, that they are lazy and indolent for the same reason that slaves are lazy and indolent, from their daily experience that all their sweat and all their labour go only to fill another man's pocket, and turn to no account to themselves. Such a consequence damps their exertions; and since they have no prospect but of continuing poor, many of them prefer, *molles in gramine somnos*, soft slumbers on the grass, to active industry that would yield them no profit. But that they are not, in general, naturally indolent, but of a character the very reverse, appears from the following circumstance, recorded by several of the statistical writers, that great numbers of them annually undertake temporary emigrations from home of 100 or 200 miles in order to get employment. Can any thing give a greater proof of the love of industry of these poor labourers, and of some great misgovernment and oppression existing at home on the part of their landlords? If those landlords would but reflect upon those emigrations, they would perceive that the disgrace of them recoils wholly upon themselves. Were hundreds of country labourers annually to quit Kent and go into Devonshire for employment, or if country labourers were to make short emigrations from Connecticut to Virginia to get work,
would

would it not be concluded that the cultivation of land met with some particular discouragement from the land owners of Kent and Connecticut. For a farm, under proper management and skilfully cultivated, ought to give employment to labourers the whole year round. Land owners, therefore, who are instrumental in the temporary emigration of their country labourers, are, in fact, contributing in so far to the diminution of their own incomes. But when they compel them by ungenerous treatment to a perpetual emigration to a foreign country, they contract a high degree of culpability in respect to the community at large. The slothful man apologizes for his indolence by saying, there is a lion in the way; but were many of the farmers in those parts to be reproached with the miserable cultivation of their fields, they would have a most solid excuse in saying there is a landlord in the way. They might justly plead, we have no property in our farms; we are in continual dread of being dispossessed; were we to attempt improvements, some avaricious neighbour, who offered a small rise of rent, would be preferred to us. These are discouragements which sink us, and are strong inducements to us to quit our native country. But we do not love to forsake our relations and friends, if we could get land to cultivate upon terms that would afford us a prospect of enjoying the fruits of our industry. As the state, by our oppression, is a very great sufferer as well as ourselves, government is therefore, for its own sake as well as ours, bound to establish a law founded on the principles of justice,

tice, by which we may be secured, that the more we improve our farms, where we were born, and which we love to occupy, the more we shall enrich ourselves. Give us but such security, and the improvements of our farms, and the embellishment of the country will in a short time prove that we are neither lazy nor unintelligent. We will then willingly participate our gains with our landlords, which will put it in their power to contribute much more largely to the defence of the state, while we ourselves, by bettering our circumstances, will be enabled to rear up new families, and to become greater customers to the manufacturers and merchants.

As the procuring the greatest quantity of produce from its lands will ever be a principal object with every wise government, and as that greatest quantity of produce cannot be procured from the lands of Great Britain, while the farmers are discouraged from improvements by want of leases, a grievance, not confined to one corner of the island alone, but pervading almost every county in the kingdom, it becomes, therefore, the duty of the legislature to impose a penalty upon those who thus obstruct the prosperity of the nation by not granting leases to their farmers; and that penalty would very properly be an additional land-tax, of six-pence in the pound, upon all lands not cultivated, under a lease of at least twenty years duration.

Should such a penalty have the happy effect of abolishing the great political evil, which now inflicts barrenness upon our lands, it may be presumed

the

the land owners would immediately from the change feel a benefit in their rents of two millions sterling annually, reckoning the cultivated acres in Great Britain at only 40 millions, and suppoſing a riſe of rent of one ſhilling per acre, upon a general introduction of leaſes. And if the land owners would be thereby benefited two millions, the national benefit thence reſulting, may conſequently be computed at four times that ſum. In point merely of profit, can the revenues of a Bengal, naturally precarious, be compared to ſuch an eaſy and permanent acquiſition within the circuit of our own ſeas. An expedient ſomewhat ſimilar to what is above propoſed was adopted by an anceſtor of the preſent King of Sardinia, who wiſhing to introduce a moſt material agricultural improvement in his dominions in Italy, impoſed a particular tax upon the lands in Piedmont; but exempted from the tax all thoſe landlords who planted upon their eſtates a certain number of mulberry trees. To this judicious law Piedmont is at preſent indebted for its annual rich revenue from the production of ſilk; for the landlords, in order to exempt themſelves from the additional land tax, made haſte to plant the ſtipulated number of mulberry trees, by which, beſides greatly benefiting their country, they quickly added very conſiderably to their own rents.

The great difficulty of forming a proper leaſe, where the advantages ariſing from improvements may be ſhared proportionately between the tenant and the landlord, has probably been one of the chief cauſes why leaſes have been ſo neglected. This difficulty, however, being

being now happily removed by the great ingenuity of the late Lord Kaims, who has given a general form of a leafe, fuited to all poffible cafes, publifhed by Dr. Anderfon in his Agricultural Report for the county of Aberdeen, and which I have added in an Appendix to my prefent difcourfe, it may therefore be expected that landlords will at length advert to the annual loffes they fuftain by not granting leafes to their farmers, and will perceive the advantages that would accrue to themfelves and the nation by cultivating their eftates by farmers excited to induftry by equitable leafes.

As men by their nature are intended to be cultivators of the ground, the more equally, therefore, they are diftributed over its furface, the greater, in all likelihood, will be their profperity. On this account the Economifts exceedingly condemn the aggregating or crowding of men, without neceffity, by twenty thoufands, and thirty thoufands, in towns and cities, and urge it as an indifpenfible duty of government to take fuch meafures as may fpread population in an equal degree over the whole territory it fuperintends, in order that men may never be far feparated from the fource from whence, as has been demonftrated, the chief of his fubfiftence and of his wealth is to originate.

There is no territory on the globe where this principle may with more propriety be reduced to practice than in this happy ifland of Great Britain; and it is a circumftance worth noting, that our anceftors two thoufand years ago, feem to have acted upon this principle from a conviction of its propriety and fuitablenefs ableness to the territory which they occupied. Julius Cæsar, in his wars on the neighbouring continent of Gaul, was employed for six or seven years, not only in fighting many battles, but besieging many populous cities, so strongly fortified by art as to seem to bid defiance to any assailant. But in Great Britain, at the same time, from his own account of it, neither walled town nor walled city seems to have existed, though in comparative populousness it appears not to have been deficient; for the infinite number of men, *hominum infinita multitudo*, which he met with in Britain, was particularly noticed by him. Indeed, this hominum infinita multitudo, or infinite number of men, is more likely to be met with in a country inhabited, without towns and cities, than in a country abounding with them; for, as in cities and towns, in general, more die than are born, their multiplicity must, therefore, rather retard population than forward it.

The dread of hostility, and the hopes of security against blood-thirsty and vagrant plunderers, were probably the motives that first drove men into walled towns, and while these motives were continually operating among the small sovereignties into which the continent was then divided, a spirit of good neighbourhood and mutual kindness seems to have prevailed among the small sovereignties into which Britain was at that time divided, and happily rendered walled towns to them unnecessary. A sense of general security against a foreign invader seems to have inspired the Britons with a sense of individual security, and with the natural concomitant of that, a
predominant

predominant paffion for rural habitation ; and this paffion fo confonant to nature, has defcended through fucceffive generations to Britons of modern times, even in fpite of the falfe policy of late years, which has given too much countenance to the augmentation of towns, from a notion that manufactures could not be properly carried on elfewhere. On the Continent, on the other hand, the natural paffion for rural habitation has through fucceffive ages continued to be in a great meafure ftifled from the want of fecurity that has always prevailed ; and one meets there not only with walled cities and walled towns, but even with walled villages.

Great Britain is now happily One and Indivifible, confequently its inhabitants, who when they lived in different fovereignties did not find cities and towns neceflary, are at prefent much lefs under any neceffity of crowding into cities and towns, from motives of defence and fecurity. Bands of ravagers are here unknown ; and individual plunderers would probably be lefs frequent, were they to exchange the wants and diftreffes of a town life for the eafily acquired competence, which honeft induftry would procure by cultivating the ground.

If cities and towns in the inland parts of Great Britain are not required for defence, a little confideration will ferve to fhew that they are not in general required for manufactures. We obferve manufactures of great extent and great ingenuity at this day carried on in villages. What, then, is to hinder all manufactures of the fame kind from being carried on the fame manner, and in many cafes, even in detached

tached hamlets. Amid all the variety of curious manufactures now carried on in Birmingham, there is hardly any one kind, that is not as completely manufactured by Mr. Bolton, in his great manufactory, at Soho, within two miles of that town, many of whose workmen, when their day's work is finished, retiring to detached hamlets on the adjoining common. If village workmen at Soho furnish the most curious hardware, we find village workmen, likewise, from the hamlets round Tunbridge Wells, furnishing the elegant cabinet work so much admired under the name of Tunbridge Ware. It is village workmen who fabricate the great variety of iron work at the very extensive manufactory at Carron. Of the great numbers of mills for spinning cotton now existing in Great Britain, many have by preference been erected in villages. In the nicest part of the linen branch, namely, damask weaving, not a few of the most skilful manufacturers are to be found in villages. Without specifying more particulars, these may suffice to shew that the great mass of manufactures may be executed by workmen not resident in towns; and from hence it follows, that it would be a true policy in Great Britain to check the augmentation of inland towns, since neither defence nor manufactures require such towns.

It is taking but a half view of things, to say, that towns give employment to the farmers; for if all those who are now workers in towns were to become workers in the country; and in general there is no natural impediment to such a transition, they would not be less consumers of the produce of the soil than at present;

present; and the same may be said of idlers in towns, were they to prefer a residence in the country. The probability rather is, that in such a state of population, both the produce of the soil would be greater, and the consumption greater; for in towns the situation of many journeymen labourers is such as prevents them from marrying, and leads them to spend many of their non-working hours in skittle-grounds or in ale houses; whereas, if those journeymen were to be settled in the country, with a garden adjoining to their house, more of them would be induced to marry, and would find delight in their hours of relaxation, in cultivating their garden, or instructing their children. Agriculture, the fountain of our wealth, would thus get a recruit of two hundred thousand new cultivators, who were they to bestow but one hour a day in field labour, would thereby more benefit the nation, than by six hours employed by them in manufactures. Were even great numbers of them to quit manufactures altogether, and to employ themselves in agriculture, the greater still would be the advantage to the nation; for the present overabundance of manufactures on one hand, and over great scarcity of products on the other, plainly shews that too many labourers are employed in the manufacturing line, and too few labourers in the agricultural line. For example, were all the cutlers in Great Britain to be idle for a couple of years, the stock in the shops gives reason to presume, that the buyers of scissars, knives, razors, &c. would during that time experience no deficiency of supply; and the same may be concluded in regard to some

other

other articles of manufacture, which the makers are frequently preffing upon the buyers at a twelve-months credit, or an eighteen months credit, a plain proof that the market is overstocked with such commodities, since the sellers of them are fain to give a premium of 6 or 7 per cent to have them taken off their hands.

How different is the state of the products of agriculture, particularly of the important article of corn! The annual supply of that article, in its greatest abundance, for these 50 years past, has never yielded a surplus of three months subsistence above the annual consumption. Nay, within these two years, the annual consumption in the article of grain has experienced a deficiency of supply of three months; so that if corn had not been brought from abroad, the whole nation must have been put for twelve months upon a short allowance of bread, with a daily diminution of one fourth of the usual quantity. The evident consequence of this seems to be, that the people of Great Britain for a long time past have gone too much into manufactures, which when sold at home produce no national income; and have bestowed too little attention upon agriculture, which in some cases has yielded the vast increase of 10,500 per cent and of which some of the products are as capable of being stored and preserved for years, as some articles of manufacture are.

The commons that require to be divided, and the waste lands that would admit of further improvement, are computed to amount in Great Britain to 22 millions of acres, which is more than one fourth

fourth of the whole territory. Thefe to be properly cultivated would give employment to 200,000 new families, and fubfiftence to twice that number; and how can they be expected to be properly cultivated unlefs inhabitants refide upon them. But befides thefe commons and wafte lands, the lands at prefent under cultivation would require many thoufands of new cultivators, in order to advance them to their higheft degree of improvement.

To accomplifh this higheft degree of improvement of our foil, the Economifts affirm, that inland towns are fo far from being neceffary, that they even obftruct it, and that the wealth and opulence of the nation would be very quickly advanced, were the hands that thofe towns have withdrawn from agriculture to be diftributed as cultivators over the whole ifland, wherever there was occafion for the fpade or the plow.

The proportionate diftribution of the people over the furface of the territory, while it greatly increafed the real and fubftantial revenue or wealth of the kingdom, would neither prejudice manufacturing induftry, nor general morals. We have feen above, that in this ifland moft extenfive branches of manufacture are carried on in villages; and as by this diftribution of the cultivators, fubfiftence would be rendered more abundant, and confequently cheaper, manufacturers would thereby naturally be drawn to intermix themfelves with them in every corner of the kingdom.

In regard to general morals it by no means follows, that if in the inland counties of Great Britain there

there were no towns befides the county town, that either rufticity or immorality would prevail. In a Chriftian country every parifh church is a centre of civilization. Chriftianity, in regard to its practical duties, is only the perfection of humanity; and whoever will attend his church, and affiduoufly practice the precepts there recommended, will neither be deficient in good morals nor in good manners. He may not have the deceitful varnifh of the late Lord Chefterfield's whited fepulchre, but he will have the polifh of the mind, which will infallibly give him a civil demeanour.

The proportionate diftribution of the people over the territory would likewife be the means of preventing innumerable expences that now detract confiderably from the nation's profperity, I mean the carriage of fubfiftence from the place where it is produced to the place where it is confumed, and of raw materials from their place of production to the place where they are manufactured; and of manufactures from the places where they are fabricated to the places where they are vended. In confequence of the prefent impolitic fyftem of people's cluftering without neceffity into large cities, or even into particular counties (for Lancafhire, we are told, contains more people than it can nourifh), cattle reared in one place are driven 300 or 400 miles to be flaughtered in another place; wool that grows in a fouthern county is carried 200 miles to be manufactured in a northern county; and when manufactured is carried many hundred miles in order to be fold. Thefe and fimilar inftances that might be produced, give employment

ployment to a great number of waggons upon our public roads, and this tranfport bufinefs paffes with many for a lucrative commerce, when it is in fact a diminution of the national profit, nearly to the amount of what it cofts. If woollen manufactures, by being fabricated where the wool is produced, were to be exempted from this charge of double tranfport, they might be bought at lower prices both by domeftic and foreign purchafers, which would promote the national profperity. If Lancafhire contains more people than it can nourifh, we ought to conclude from thence, either that the cultivation of that county is not brought to its higheft degree of improvement, or that the county is too populous, in which laft cafe, it would be a national advantage, if the fupernumerary inhabitants were to remove to fome other part of the ifland, where there is a deficiency of population, and a fuperfluity of fubfiftence. The cattle that are now driven at a confiderable expence 300 or 400 miles to be flaughtered, might more profitably to the nation be confumed near the fpots where they are reared, were thofe fpots to have their proportionate fhare of cultivators and manufacturers.

Although large cities and large towns in the inland parts of Great Britain may juftly be confidered as detracting from the nations profperity, they would however have a direct contrary effect when fituated upon the coafts of the ifland. As much as villages and detached hamlets ought to be preferred in the interior of the ifland, fo much ought walled cities and

and walled towns to be encouraged upon its coasts, and at the mouths of its navigable rivers. There, and there only, walled cities and walled towns ought to be as numerous as possible, on many accounts, but principally for the three following reasons.

First, numerous walled towns upon its coasts would be the means of promoting and extending foreign commerce, which though no great source of income, compared with agriculture, yet when conducted with prudence, may add something to the enjoyments as well as to the riches of the inhabitants.

Secondly, numerous walled towns upon the coasts would contribute greatly to the increase of the fishery, that golden mine to those who prosecute it with skill and industry. The British seas are an undivided common, remarkable for its great fertility, and they who cultivate this common, namely, fishermen, ought naturally to have their habitations on the edge of it. As it would be absurd to expect a constant resident in a large town to be a farmer, so it would be equally absurd to expect the inhabitant remote from the coast to be a fisherman. How many thousands in this island follow a marine life hardly for any other reason but because they have been born and bred within sight of the sea. Were the number of those in Great Britain born and bred within sight of the sea, to be then twenty times as great as it is at present, it might be expected that those following a marine life would also be twenty times as numerous. In proportion to the harvest, so should be the reapers. Since the British seas can furnish twenty times the wealth or sub-
fiftence

fiftence that is at prefent extracted from them, it will therefore be a prudent policy in the government of Britain to adopt fuch means as may augment the number of thofe following a marine life twenty fold. And what policy could fo much augment the number of thofe who follow a marine life, as to induce a million more of inhabitants to refide on the fea coafts, by giving every encouragement to multiply maritime cities. The Penfionary De Witt, in his Political Maxims, p. 35, computes the number of the people in the United Provinces at 2,400,000, and of thefe he reckons 450,000 *earn their living by the fifheries at fea, and fetting them out with fhips, rigging, cafks, falt, and other materials or inftruments, and the traffic that depends thereon.* In another place he fays, *more than the one half of the trade of Holland would decay, in cafe the trade of fifh were deftroyed.* In a population of 2,400,000 fouls, 450,000 make near a fifth part, and in that proportion the number of people in Great Britain depending for a fubfiftence upon the fifhing bufinefs, and what relates to it ought to amount to near two millions, were the views of government, and the views of individuals, turned as earneftly to that great object in Britain as they are in Holland, and that they are not fo turned, is no fmall reproach to the policy of this ifland; for what has maintained this fifth part of the inhabitants of Holland, has been drawn from feas properly belonging to Great Britain; or from feas fituated more conveniently for Britifh fifhermen, han for Dutch fifhermen; and capable of maintaining

taining ten times more people than who now draw their subsistence from them. Had Britain even but a small sea frontier to improve, the neglect of improving it, though not of great consequence, would still be a blameable policy. But Great Britain, including Ireland, (which I mean to be included in all that is said, or shall be said in this discourse) has the advantage of a sea frontier of upwards of 3000 miles, and of seas washing that frontier, affording subsistence for millions of men, were those millions to be induced by political regulations to cultivate them. Should a rich proprietor possess an immense plain of great fertility to the extent of 30,000 or 40,000 acres, where the herbage, as in some places of Hungary, rises to the heighth of five or six feet, and should he nevertheless keep neither bullock nor horse upon it, nor any live stock whatever, it would be concluded by the sensible and judicious, that such proprietor had not his eyes open to his own interest. But must not the same thing be concluded of the people of Great Britain and Ireland, who continue to give so little attention to the watery plain with which they are surrounded, though an hundred times more to be valued on account of the wealth it would afford, than such a plain as is above mentioned.

The first and most natural step to the improvement of this watery plain is by encouragements to bring multitudes of men to live within view of it; for it is hardly possible for multitudes of men to live constantly within view of it, without a great part

of

of them forming such a connection with it, as may procure them, if not opulence, at least a subsistence. Were the proposition of founding either a second Birmingham or a second Liverpool to be deliberated upon, true policy would decidedly declare in favour of the new Liverpool, because all the arts, trades, and manufactures carried on in Birmingham, or in any inland town whatever, might just as conveniently be carried on in the new maritime city, with the addition of the trades that seafaring business creates.

But instead of one new Liverpool, the sea frontier of Great Britain and Ireland would admit of twenty new Liverpools, which so far from diminishing the national population, would contribute greatly to augment it. How many vacant and desart spots are there at present on the shores of these islands, where such new maritime cities might conveniently be founded, were Government to make it an object of its attention to mark out such spots, and give encouragement to new settlers to inhabit them. The situations for such new maritime cities ought not to be hastily chosen, nor fixed upon entirely upon the report of military engineers. Civil engineers ought also to be consulted, and the reports of both to be compared and weighed. The great abundance of fish ought to be a leading motive for fixing the situation of many of the new maritime cities in their vicinity, and such is that abundance in our north-western seas, that a city of 8,000 or 10,000 inhabitants might be supported by fishing, fifhing, and the commerce depending upon it, on many of the now half inhabited iflands on the weft coaft of Scotland*

Building in thefe new maritime cities might probably foon become a profitable fpeculation, as government, it may be hoped, will ere long have a happy opportunity of colonizing them with 150,000 or 200,000 men, who by changing their fwords and cutlaffes for plows and fifhing nets, may add to the wealth of the country, and at the fame time may continue to add to its ftrength.

The public encouragements to thefe new fettlers may be various. Were the tax upon bricks, ufed in their buildings, to be remitted to them, the general amount of that tax would probably thereby not be diminifhed. The fame might be faid of the general amount of the houfe-tax, and of the win-

---

* In the northern counties and iflands of Scotland are reckoned 4,528,000, and the population in 1795 was computed to be 137,754 fouls, which is near 38 acres to each individual, or about 20 fouls to a fquare mile. In the kingdom of Naples the general population is reckoned to give 203 fouls to a fquare mile, fupported by the fertility of the territory. The land in the north part of Scotland is grealy inferior to that of the kingdom of Naples in point of fertility; but this inferiority is fully compenfated by the fuperior fertility of the feas in furnifhing fubfiftence to man; therefore the improvement of the fifheries by the eftablifhment of large maritime towns may render the lands in thofe parts of the ifland capable of fupporting a population equal to that of the kingdom of Naples, that is, would increafe the number of their inhabitants to near a million and an half, and the value of the lands in a proportionable degree.

dow-tax, were the new settlers to be exempted from those taxes for ten years. Premiums might likewise be bestowed on those who built or navigated boats or vessels of a certain tonnage, or spun twine to a certain quantity.

These indulgencies, without being at all burdensome to government, or sensibly diminishing the general sum total of the taxes, would be most alluring inducements to draw inhabitants to the new settlements, who by directing their industry without delay to fishing, and the seafaring business dependant upon it, would as assuredly acquire an income as if they were to become farmers in any county of Great Britain. They ought for the first years to receive every prudential support, which, in the succession of time, they would most amply repay to the nation. Though an orchard does not yield any fruit sufficient to defray the expence of forming it, till several years after it is planted, yet that does not deter the prudent husbandman from incurring that expence. In like manner though these new settlements should for some years yield little return in point of taxes, yet the prudent statesman will not refuse to them his fostering care, knowing that, with proper management, their natural advantages will enable them not only to subsist, but to acquire opulence, and consequently to be large contributors to the public supply. There was a time when the immense capitals possessed by the wealthy inhabitants of Liverpool, Newcastle, Glasgow, &c. did not exist; but in the same manner as these capitals have been created, so might capitals be formed in

the

the new maritime cities, since they would be equally favoured by the ocean as Liverpool, Newcastle, or Glasgow. How have the capitals of our great West Indian planters been formed but by producing with great labour, and sending to market an article of very general consumption? But fish is a commodity not of more limited consumption than sugar, with this superior advantage, that besides the foreign sale, it actually makes great part of the subsistence of those who produce it and send it to market. As the market for both is daily increasing, colonizing on our own coasts may be found to be as true policy as colonizing in the West Indies.

A third principal reason for multiplying cities and towns upon our coasts is, that they would in such situations add much more essentially both to the defensive and offensive strength of the nation. I have said that Great Britain and Ireland have the advantage of a sea frontier upwards of 3,000 miles in extent; but while this frontier shall remain but thinly occupied by inhabitants, it will be more consonant to truth to say, Great Britain and Ireland have the disadvantage of a sea frontier upwards of 3,000 miles in extent, because from this very extent a foreign invader may assail them in a greater number of points. But were a foreign invader to know, that he could no where land within 100 miles of the seat of government of either island, without having a populous and regularly fortified city to attack, or without having within 20 miles of him two such cities on the coast, that could each send out a military force of 10,000 men, we may be almost

most sure, that a fleet could hardly be wanted for the defence of such a coast, or at least it may be affirmed, that a coast so peopled and so fortified, would be twice as formidable to a foreign enemy, as if left unpeopled and unfortified to the protection of a fleet alone.

Independent then of the extension of foreign commerce, and of the extension of the fishery, the cheap defence of the kingdom calls loudly for the multiplication of maritime cities of great populousness and great strength. It is hardly in the nature of things that such cities should be filled with idlers; and the example of Holland shews us that where manufacturing and commercial industry prevails, one great and populous city does not prevent another great and populous city from thriving within twenty miles of it, nay sometimes within ten miles. In this view it may be affirmed, that two new Liverpools might arise on the coast of Essex, between Harwich and South End, at the mouth of the Thames, and twice as many on the coasts of Kent and Sussex. These, when strongly fortified, would be most powerful outguards to the metropolis; and it may be presumed that in the policy of having such outguards originated the privileges conferred upon the cinque ports, which in former ages, during the weak state of the naval force of Europe, well acquitted themselves by their services to the public. But instead of having only cinque ports, or five sea ports, true policy in these modern times demands that Great Britain and Ireland should have an hundred sea ports, or maritime cities,

cities, flourishing in populousness, and so fortified as to bid defiance to a sudden attack of an invading enemy. In the new maritime cities, founded on the coasts of Essex, Kent, and Sussex, might be carried on to greater national advantage many branches of manufacture and seafaring business, now most unnecessarily established in London and its vicinity. As neither corn nor coals are staples of the port of London, it is a heedless policy to suffer distilleries, iron founderies, fire engines, and other works and undertakings that require a great consumption of fuel to be concentered in the capital, as though they could prosper no where but on the banks of the Thames. All these, instead of being crowded into London, should studiously be removed from it, and might be carried on as profitably for the proprietors, if not more profitably, on the shores of Essex, Kent, and Sussex. Thither likewise a great part of the ship building business, that may now be said to encumber the river Thames, might with national advantage be transferred. And with national advantage likewise the overgrown metropolis with its neighbourhood could spare thousands and ten thousands for the peopling of these new cities, which might also attract great numbers of inhabitants with large capitals from the opposite continent, were the impolitic restrictions against foreigners to be removed, and succeeded by invitations. Men of mercantile enterprise are often of more consequence to the aggrandisement and prosperity of a commercial city, than even a good situation or a good harbour. What then might be expected

pected were thefe three circumftances to be united, and to all appearance it remains only with our legiflature to unite them. Nature has already given us the two former, and were our legiflature to invite foreigners to fettle in thofe cities, by the offer of naturalization, thoufands of them would probably prefer the fecurity and quiet to be obtained on the fhores of Great Britain, to the infecurity and oppreffion to which they are but too often expofed on the continent.

But without enlarging further, my readers may eafily figure to themfelves, from the preceding illuftrations, what would be the natural and happy confequence of the eftablifhment of the fyftem of the Economifts, in refpect to Great Britain and Ireland. The lands of both iflands would be cultivated under leafes upon the model of that of Lord Kaimes, by which the farmers would be excited to increafe the national produce in the full fecurity of augmenting their own incomes. Manufacturers, without expecting any income from them, would be cherifhed on account of the multiplied conveniences arifing from them. Taxes upon confumption would in general be abolifhed; and the fupply for national defence would, as formerly, be drawn directly from the national income by a fingle tax upon the furplus of that income, poffeffed by the land proprietors. What alone fuftains the whole of the people would be allowed to fuffice for fuftaining the defenders of the people, who, when defenders, do not ceafe to make part of that whole. The real refources of the nation would be underftood by the

ge-

generality of the people to confift in the productions of the foil, and not in ftampt paper, which would animate their zeal to favour the increafe of thofe productions. Abundance would be attended with its natural confequence cheapnefs, and cheapnefs would greatly extend the circle of our foreign commerce. Gold and filver would become the general medium of circulation, and few families be without fome referve of them, either in coin or in plate. The hamlets and villages would be fo multiplied in the interior parts, that in every county a traveller would never lofe fight of one habitation before he might fee another, each the feat of induftry, and many of them the nurferies of numerous and healthy children; and the fea frontier would be every where fpiked, or, in the French idiom, *briftled* with large and populous cities, abounding with fifhermen, failors, and artifts of every kind, and fo fortified with rampart and ditch, as to bid defiance to the fudden attack of a foreign invader.

APPENDIX.

APPENDIX.

A GENERAL PLAN OF A LEASE

BY

LORD KAIMS,

WITH

SOME REMARKS UPON IT BY DR. ANDERSON,

IN HIS

AGRICULTURAL REPORT FOR THE COUNTY OF ABERDEEN.

I AM extremely happy to have it in my power on this occasion to lay before the public at large, through means of the Honourable Board, to whom this report is addressed, a plan of a lease which is perfectly adapted to secure alike the interest of the tenant, and the legitimate rights of the landlord; by which the rights of humanity can never be violated, and which can apply to all possible cases, so that neither of the parties can ever acquire an undue advantage over the other in any situation of things. To effect all these things appeared to me, for a great many years, to exceed the powers of human ingenuity to devise. It has been done; and the public are obliged to the late Lord Kaims for this excellent device.

His

APPENDIX.

His lordship proposed that the lease should extend to an indefinite number of years consisting of fixed periods, at the end of each of which a rise of rent should take place, with permission for the tenant, at the period of each of these rises of rent, to give up his farm, if he shall see proper, and granting a similar power to the landlord, upon proper terms, to resume his land if he shall think fit. The particulars of this contract, and the grounds on which they rest, are as under:

He assumes it as a postulatum that a landlord and tenant are capable of forming a tolerably just estimate of the value of land in question for a short period of years, such as it is customary to grant leases for in Scotland: say 21 years. And having agreed upon these terms, which for the present we shall call 100l. rent, the tenant expresses a wish to have his lease extended to a longer period. To this the proprietor objects, on this ground, that it is not possible to form a precise estimate of what the value of the ground may be at the end of that period. He has already seen that ground, for the last 21 years, has increased much more in value than any person at the beginning of that period could easily have conceived it would have done, and therefore he cannot think of giving it off just now for a longer period, as a similar rise in value may be expected to take place in future. This reasoning appears to be well founded, and therefore to give the landlord a reasonable gratification, he proposes that it should be stipulated that if the tenant should agree to give a certain rise of rent, at the end of that period,

APPENDIX.

riod, fuppofe 20l. the landlord fhould confent that the leafe fhould run on for another period of 21 years; unlefs in the cafes to be after mentioned.

But as it may happen that this 20l. now ftipulated to be paid at fo diftant a period, may be more than the farmer will find he is able to pay, an option fhall be given to him to refign his leafe, if he fhould find that is the cafe, by giving the landlord legal notice, one year at leaft, before the expiration of the leafe; but if that notice be omitted thus to be given, it fhall be underftood that the tenant is bound to hold the leafe for the fecond 21 years, at the rent fpecified in the contract. And if the landlord does not give the tenant warning within one month after the period, it fhall be underftood that he too is bound to accept of the ftipulated additional rent for the 21 years that are to fucceed.

It may however alfo happen that the fum fpecified in the leafe may be a rent confiderably below the then prefent value of the farm; or the proprietor may have very ftrong reafons for wifhing to refume the poffeffion of that land, or to obtain an adequate rent for it: a power therefore fhould be given to him, in either cafe, to refume the lands, if he fhould fo incline. But as a great part of that prefent value may be owing to the exertions of the farmer, who has laid out money upon the farm, in hopes to enjoy it for a fecond period of 21 years, it would be unjuft to deprive him of this benefit, without giving him a valuable confideration for that improved value. On this account it fhould be ftipulated, that in cafe the proprietor at this time

refume

resume the farm, he shall become bound to pay to the tenant ten years purchase of the additional rent he had agreed to pay; which in the example above stated would be 200l.

But the land may be worth still more than the 20l. of rise mentioned in the lease, and the tenant may be content to pay more, say 10l. rather than remove, and he makes offer accordingly to do so. In that case the landlord should be bound either to accept that additional offer, or to pay *ten* years purchase for that also; and so on for every other offer the tenant shall make, before he agrees to move from the farm.

In this way the landlord is always certain that he can never be precluded from obtaining the full value for his land, whatever circumstances may arise. And if the tenant shall prove disagreeable, so that he would wish rather to put another in his place upon the same terms, it never can be any hardship upon the landlord to pay the stipulated sum; because it would be the same thing to him as if he bought a new estate at ten years purchase, free of taxes: a thing he can never expect to do. It is indeed true that it would be more advantageous for him to allow the present tenant to continue; and therefore this alternative will be always, unless in very extraordinary cases, accepted of, as it ever ought to be; and thus the tenant's mind is impressed with a conviction that he will continue in his possession: a conviction that ought ever to prevail, because it stimulates to industry in the highest degree. And as the tenant is thus certain that, at the very worst, his family must be entitled to

draw

draw a reafonable remuneration for the exertions of his induftry, he can never find the fmalleft tendency to flacken his endeavours in any way.

By ftipulating in the original leafe in the fame manner, that at the end of the fecond 21 years, the leafe fhall be continued for 21 years more, and fo on at the end of the third, and fourth, and any farther numbers of periods of 21 years, on agreeing to pay a fpecified rife of rent; referving to each party the fame privileges as above defcribed, the leafe might be continued to perpetuity, without either party ever being in danger of having an undue advantage over the other. The tenant will always be certain of having a preference given him over every other perfon, and will of courfe go on with unceafing exertions to better his land, which will of neceffity tend to augment the income of the proprietor much more than could have happened under any other fyftem of management.

Such are the outlines of that plan of a leafe his Lordfhip has propofed. By this plan the tenant's hands are not tied up by reftrictive claufes dictated by ignorance, under the pretext of fecuring the intereft of the landlord. His intereft is fecured in a much more effectual manner, while the tenant is left at full liberty to avail himfelf of his knowledge, his fkill, and his induftry. Inftead of ceafing to begin any arduous undertaking, as he ever muft do where he has no leafe, or of beginning to improve for a few years only at the commencement of his leafe, but flopping in a fhort while in the midft of his career, and then running it down

to

to the same exhausted state as it was at its commencement, he continues to push forward without ever stopping, and advances even with an accelerated progress for an endless period of years. No person but an experienced farmer can conceive the difference that would be between the productiveness of the same land under this management, at the end of an hundred years, from what it would have been if let even for detached periods of 21 years each. In unimproved waste lands, the difference would approach to infinity. In lands which were originally very rich, the difference would be less considerable; but in all cases where cultivation could take place the difference would be very great. It is worth remarking here also, that if this arrangement were adopted, a new order of men in civil society would be created, different from any that at present exists. They would be inferior in point of rank to that class of men who are called *gentlemen*; and superior in point of wealth and energy, not only to the present order of *farmers*, but even to that class of men who are called *yeomen*. The peculiar political advantage attached to this order of society would be, that while their exertions would always insure affluence, that affluence never would become such as to permit them, by imitating the life of the higher orders, to neglect their own proper concerns; for the moment they did so, their exertions in business would become slackened, in consequence of which they could not afford such a rent as others around them would be willing to give, and so they must quit their lease.

Here

Here we are led to perceive the moſt eſſential difference between thus granting what may almoſt be called a perpetual leaſe, and every other *long* leaſe that ever yet has been tried; for in all other long leaſes, if the rent ſtipulated at firſt ſhall prove to be at laſt inadequate, and the holder of the leaſe be reduced to poverty, by diſſipation or otherwiſe, he may neither himſelf be able to cultivate the ground properly, nor can another be permitted to do ſo; and by this means the proprietor may not only be for a long period of years deprived of an adequate value for his land, but that land alſo being locked up from improvement, may be doomed long to remain in a degree of comparative ſterility. Nothing of that kind could here happen.

It differs alſo very much from that ſort of tenure which is called yeomanry, in which the ſmall capital, if properly applied, would have been juſt ſufficient to give ſcope for agricultural exertions, but by being locked up on the original purchaſe of the land, it deprives the poſſeſſor of the only funds he had in his power to apply for improving his land. Inſtead of active exertions, and chearful affluence through life, he is thus ſtinted in every exertion, and is doomed to a perpetual hard ſtruggle againſt the harraſſments of poverty.

In ſhort, were I either a proprietor or a tenant, I ſhould either let or take land upon theſe terms, in preference to any other I have ever heard of. Several little clauſes have been overlooked by his Lordſhip, which it would be neceſſary to advert to. Some proviſion ought to be made reſpecting trees on

a leaſe

a leafe of this kind, as it is probable the tenant might find it convenient to plant, which by the common law of Scotland he cannot do at prefent with a view to profit. Perhaps the wood, if any was on the farm at the time of his entry, ought to be valued, and he fhould be bound to leave at leaft an equal value upon it, or pay the balance. Whatever timber trees he himfelf had planted, he fhould be at liberty to cut at pleafure, for the ufe of the farm, unlefs it were fuch individual trees as the landlord, from fituation or other caufes, fhould think proper to mark for refervation. He fhould alfo have permiffion to fell fuch trees as he inclined, unlefs as above referved, or during the laft fix years of any of the 21 years of the leafe. But in cafe of his removal, the proprietor fhall either permit him the whole of the trees that was over the value of the ftock at his entry, or take the whole, or fuch part as he chofe to referve, at an appreciated value. In cafe of his removal alfo the tenant fhould be bound not to outlabour the ground, during the laft fix years of the leafe, or to crop it improperly, or to carry off any ftraw or dung: otherwife to pay the damages that fhould thus accrue to the landlord, at the eftimate of two honeft men, to be mutually chofen; and to leave the houfes in a habitable condition, and the fences in good repair. There feems to be no other claufe neceffary in fuch a leafe.

FINIS.